Praise for *Room at the Table*

"As new and seasoned Disciples of Christ ... their history, they will find a jewel in P... m-plicated, conversational ...d information inside these ... know the fullness of this c... have been available in diffe... ...ut this volume brings the varied pai... ...ys them side-by-side. Rev. Jha's theological ins... ...hallenges the reader to make the connections between and absorb the lessons of these once disconnected and often overlooked perspectives on our national and church history. This book provides a solid foundation for learning a fuller Disciples history than was possible before. It is also a launching pad for more history to be unearthed...and created, by challenging us all to work toward a true welcome table."

Ayanna Johnson, First Vice Moderator,
Christian Church (Disciples of Christ)

"I find this book filling a void that has plagued Disciples of Christ for decades. Yes, the documents that contained this vital information were there, but Sandhya Jha has now assembled parts of them into a coherent and flowing narrative of a side of Disciples history that had simply been overlooked by too many for too long. Reasons could be given for that ignoring—the point now is that we can no longer ignore this and pretend to be a whole people. I commend her for her disciplined work and recommend this reading to every person who really loves the Disciples' inclusiveness of which we speak and which can become reality. This goal must begin with the knowledge of our story. Here, now, is a critical part."

Chris Hobgood, former General Minister and President of the
Christian Church (Disciples of Christ)

"We must learn from history if we are to understand the present and have a better future. In the present of the Christian Church (Disciples of Christ), diversity is a vital reality—racial-ethnic diversity in particular. In the future, such diversity will only gain in import as the church strives mightily to achieve its vision as a true Christian community that demonstrates a passion for justice. But for some time, Disciples have found it difficult to come to grips with that diversity, which has been with them since the beginning of their movement. This difficulty stemmed in part from lack of an accessible history of so-called people of color in the communion. With the publication of this book, Rev. Sandhya R. Jha has done a great service for all Disciples and for anybody interested in the history of racial-ethnic minorities in a mainline denomination in North America. As Rev. Jha acknowledges, the book is an initial telling of a complicated story—at times dismaying, at times inspiring. But throughout she tells it with candor, verve, and a theological point of view."

Timothy S. Lee, Director of Asian (Korean) Church Studies Program at Brite Divinity School, Texas Christian University

"For too many years the Christian Church (Disciples of Christ) in the United States and Canada has struggled to discern God's will for us as church, particularly as it relates to 'people of color.' Over the many years as the church was founded, became a 'movement' and finally a denomination, it has struggled with the place of people of color in that makeup. Sandyha in her literary wisdom has been able to capture in a nutshell the journey of our church, including the African American, the Latino Hispanic, the American Asian Pacific Islander, and the Haitian's struggles to identify completely what each of our cultures brings to the 'Lord's Table.' This book is an offering to the whole church that recounts briefly the journey of each racial ethnic group in trying to reach full recognition, participation and inclusiveness in the church we love and want to see move forward."

Luis E. Ferrer, honorary National Hispanic Pastor and retired Disciples minister

ROOM at the TABLE

*Struggle for Unity and Equality
in Disciples History*

SANDHYA RANI JHA

CHALICE
PRESS
ST. LOUIS, MISSOURI

Bible quotations, unless otherwise noted, are from the *New Revised Standard Version Bible,* copyright 1989, Division of Christian Education of the National Council of the Churches of Christ in the United States of America. Used by permission. All rights reserved.

Cover and interior design: Elizabeth Wright

Visit Chalice Press on the World Wide Web at
www.chalicepress.com

10 9 8 7 6 5 4 3 2 1   09 10 11 12 13 14

Library of Congress Cataloging-in-Publication Data

Jha, Sandhya R.
  Room at the table : the struggle for unity and equality in Disciple's history / by Sandhya Rani Jha.
    p. cm.
  ISBN 978-0-8272-3656-1
  1. Disciples of Christ–History. I. Title.

  BX7315.J46 2009
  286.6'3–dc22

                                                    2009008691

Printed in the United States of America

Contents

Foreword

El Día del Hombre
Por Lucas Torres

Hay que trasponer muchas fronteras.
Marchemos.
Los viejos clarines duermen
sueno de mudez y herrumbre.
No importa, marchemos.
Que ya la aurora nos hiere;
Que ya en sangre de palabras
se nos coagula el tiempo.
Noches hay en que la luna
ha alumbrado el pensamiento.
Lo que dijimos entonces
Era un prado de silencio.
Nos ha llegado la hora del
fragor y el grito,
Hora que repercute por las
hondonadas de nuestro nombre.
Henos aquí; marchemos.
Es el día del hombre.

The Day of Man*

By Lucas Torres

Many frontiers must be overcome–
Let us march.
The old trumpets sleep
a dream of rust and stillness.
It matters not; let us march.
Already the dawn strikes us;
Already in the blood of words
our time is clotted.
There were nights in which the
moon illumned [sic] our thought.
What we said then
Was a meadow of silence.
The hour of clash and outcry
has come–
The hour that rings in the
depths of our Name.
We are here; let us march.
It is the day of man!

---

*Originally published in *The Disciple* (February 17, 1974): 19. Part of the descriptor beneath the poem read: "A recognized poet, Mr. Torres speaks in "El Dia del Hombre" of the new hope surging through Latin America. His poem has veen [sic] translated for *The Disciple* by Argelia Colón and William J. Nottingham." Lucas Torres died in November 2008. He was national pastor emeritus for Hispanic Ministries, Christian Church (Disciples of Christ).

Acknowledgments

This book has been long in the making. I submit it with humble thanks to the Disciples Historical Society for their willingness to help a non-historian piece together a rarely-told history; and with thanks to Kristine Culp at Disciples Divinity House in Chicago, who told me to do something when I complained about the lack of acknowledgment of people of color in our Disciples History and Thought classes. I also submit it with thanks to the Disciples historian who recognizes that White Disciples history cannot be told without understanding its interplay with these stories, so that the next history of the Christian Church (Disciples of Christ) is a whole history.

Finally, I write this for the Disciples who will make this church better than my generation has–the NAPAD, Convocation, and Convention youth, as well as your White sisters and brothers who continue the struggle to get us closer to the realm of God here on earth: a realm of dignity, compassion and just peace.

Latinas joined a church eager to engage in missions in Spanish-speaking countries, but uncomfortable ministering with or even acknowledging the ministries of Spanish-speaking Americans. Asians found Christ through a church that never spoke out against discriminatory immigration acts that buffeted their communities whenever their labor had been extracted. This book is an effort at sharing a small part of these stories.

Theologians use the fancy word *hermeneutics* to describe the lens through which we view things. We do not (at least I do not) study history just "so we do not repeat it." We study history because it tells us something about who we are now and what we can be. We can read the history of the Christian Church (Disciples of Christ) in relation to people of color in a few different ways. We can read it through the lens of "critical distance," where we look at the facts and add them to the database in our minds; but we don't experience their realities within ourselves—feeling unmoved by or disconnected from the stories—as if they don't really have anything to do with us. We can read Disciples history through a lens of self-righteousness: "Weren't the early Disciples awful? Thank God we're not like that now!" We can read it through a lens of resistance, angry that history has been dug up to create barriers between people who would otherwise have gotten along. Or we can read it with openness to what this past means in terms of why we function as a church (and churches) the way we do today, and whether we are satisfied with that. We cannot change the past, but we can learn about our present by knowing our past better.

I have heard on more than one occasion that people of color make far too big a fuss about being different when we should all just get along and focus on what unites us. The object of this book is to look at why those distinctions between communities might have occurred, and to examine our stories as a relevant part of the whole story of the Disciples. Ultimately, it is my hope we can have a conversation about unity in diversity that does not require anyone—Latino/a, Black, White, Asian, Native American, Haitian—to deny the challenges to (as well as the resistance that made possible) the thriving Christian unity movement that we have all chosen to call home.

History often validates the reality of persons and a people. So far, the histories of the Disciples have told mostly the stories of White Disciples. The colorful and often-controversial churchman and Black historian, Merle R. Eppse, said, "Black Disciples of Christ history exists like African stories—in the mind of those who have heard about or experienced the event."[1] This book is a first effort to tell these stories that so few of us know so that our larger church may benefit. Let us pray that we can receive each other's stories, so that we may be more wholly the Disciples that our forebears desired us all to be.

One final caveat—much has been written to heroize the White founders and White church leaders who built the brotherhood that is the Christian Church (Disciples of Christ). Sometimes it may feel as if this book contradicts those accounts. Let me be clear; both realities stand side-by-side. Their failures do not erase their earnest desire to do God's will any more than our failures erase our desire to serve Christ in the world. This is just another part of the story.

Notes

[1]William K. Fox, "Before You Begin," *The Untold Story: A Short History of Black Disciples* (St. Louis: Christian Board of Publication, 1976), 4.

1

A "First-Century" Nineteenth-Century Church

The Beginnings of the Disciples to the End of the Civil War

The founders of the Christian Church (Disciples of Christ) proclaimed themselves a "first-century church." By this, they meant to distance themselves from all of the clutter Christianity had picked up in the 1700 years following Jesus' death. They desired a pristine church: a church relying exclusively on the Holy Scriptures to offer them direction, a church that allowed regular people to interpret those Scriptures, and a church that did not require a particular creed in order for people to experience the Lord's Supper.

Ignore for a moment that the New Testament indicates a diversity of first-century churches, none of them pristine or without conflict.[1] Something the founding Disciples ignored was that their world was different from the world of first-century Palestine. The United States of America was a nation of immigrants in which some Christians considered certain people less than human, a nation claiming its role in "civilizing" and "Christianizing" others as it took their land, a nation that demanded cheap labor from other countries but did not acknowledge the human dignity of the laborers. That nation would shape a different church than the church that Peter and Paul grew. Because many of their convictions ignored their contemporary context, the founders' "first-century church" would not be able to avoid many conflicts around the clash of their dream with the concrete reality of their time. As the first denomination founded on American soil, the Disciples' story follows many of the contours of the story of the United States.

According to one writer (and many Disciples historians concur), the Christian Church (Disciples of Christ) was a distinctly American church in its makeup from the very beginning. The frontier did not welcome the old, established churches of the old world, and "by the year 1800, scarcely ten percent of the population belonged to any church."[2] Guin Stemmler goes on to say, "The kind of religious ideas embraced by Thomas and Alexander Campbell and Barton W. Stone would not have been possible anywhere except in a new world where there were no precedents, no 'good old days' to imitate. Each person was free to follow the guidance of his own conscience and to interpret the Bible for himself."[3]

This focus on individualism and unity creates a tension in the Christian Church (Disciples of Christ) that one can observe in the complex relationship of the mostly-White church with its racial-ethnic ministries throughout its history.

Since Disciples history followed the White settlers' path westward across the country, its earliest days had little interaction with Latinos and Latinas (more prominent in the Southwest and later in the century as part of the Christian Church's mission work abroad) or with Asians (again part of the story of the western United States and beyond). Nineteenth-century slavery, a considerably different institution than the forms of slavery and servitude that existed in the first century, provided the context and confronted the founders within their unified, "first-century church." It is fairly safe to say that for as long as there have been Disciples, there have been Disciples of color. Two of the Christian Church's earliest congregations–in Cane Ridge, Kentucky and Brush Run, Pennsylvania–listed African Americans on the membership rolls as early as 1820.[4] Some people today bemoan that early on the Christian Church (Disciples of Christ) was able to bring together people across racial lines; but then people of color left the White churches, abandoning Christ's vision of an integrated church. The reality of those golden days, however, is a little more complex. This book reminds us that sometimes we rose to the core values of our denomination, sometimes we failed, and on some occasions those core values were insufficient to mobilize action on behalf of the realm of God.

In slave states, Blacks first entered Disciples churches as slaves of church members. In some churches, they were allowed to join while remaining slaves. Sometimes they were allowed to worship in the same building. One prime example is the church at Midway, Kentucky, where Blacks were allowed to worship in the balcony, which was more of a hay loft; it had no stairwell. So in order to worship, Black members climbed a ladder into the balcony. However, the balcony was later removed. At this point Black members founded the Colored Christian Church of Midway, Kentucky (later Second Christian Church). Constituted in 1854, the church was the first African American congregation in the Christian Church (Disciples of Christ) movement.[5] Alexander Campbell, a slave who converted to Christianity during the Cane Ridge revival, helped establish the church. He was such an excellent preacher that the Kentucky Missionary Society purchased his freedom for $1,000. [6] It took Campbell another three years to earn the money needed to free his wife.

In addition to the second-class seating of Black Disciples in slave states, their opportunities for leadership in the "priesthood of all believers" likewise were limited in title, function, and to whom they could minister. According to William Fox, a prominent Black Disciples historian until his death in 2004, "In mixed congregations, offices open to African Americans were those of exhorters (talented persons ordained to preach to African Americans), deacons who served African Americans, and custodians. In separate congregations there also were elders and board members."[7]

Slave states were not the only ones that had Black Christians or Black Christian Churches, however. While White "mother" churches usually supervised Black churches in slave states, Black Christian Churches in the North functioned autonomously. Notions of congregational autonomy, core to the understandings of the early church, meant that the church's position on "political" issues such as slavery was profoundly mixed. "Disciples of Christ made no dramatic witness during the Civil War," noted Disciples historian Kenneth Henry, "and tended to conform to the prevailing views wherever they were located: in the North there were Disciple abolitionists, and in the South there were pro-slavery advocates. Consequently, Disciple programs to aid the freedmen were ... dependent upon local initiative of dedicated individuals."[8] While secondary sources[9] tell us as much about the time they were written as the time they write about, it is interesting to note that one mini-history of the Disciples written in the 1950s observed almost with celebration that:

> During the 1850's the slavery issue divided both the nation and many American churches. The Methodists, Baptists, and Presbyterians split officially. But the Christian Churches or Disciples of Christ, who were nearly equal in numbers in the North and South, did not divide over the issue. All political and social questions were considered as belonging to the realm, not of necessary faith, but of opinion where people could differ without dividing the church.[10]

The Christian Church (Disciples of Christ) was founded in the midst of one of America's most conflicted moments.

Alexander Campbell mingled a focus on the eschaton[11] with a focus on political realism. So, it is not surprising that while he ultimately freed his own slaves, Campbell wrote in a *Millennial Harbinger* article published in September 1851:

> Christians should submit to every ordinance of man for the Lord's sake ... Christian congregations are not called upon to carry their resolutions and enactments beyond their own immediate congregation ... slavery cannot be abolished unilaterally by the North, nor by abolitionists anywhere ... (Slavery) can be abolished only by one of two ways: by amalgamation or colonization abroad, or in some portion of our own country, exclusively given to them.[12]

It has been posited that Campbell was so concerned about division within the restorationist movement[13] that he did not want to promote division in the North-South alliance (in contrast, says John Hull of Bethany College, to the Congregationalists—now United Church of Christ—whose northeastern stronghold allowed them more freedom to respond to slavery).

Interestingly, several of Campbell's siblings were active in the Underground Railroad. His sister Jane McKeever and her husband, Matthew, were described as "the rankest kind of abolitionist and never hesitated to denounce slavery as an abomination."[14] In celebrating the publication of the North-Western Christian Magazine, an abolitionist magazine for members of the restorationist movement, she wrote:

> I truly rejoice to find that ONE of our brotherhood [referring to the editor] has had the fortitude, and (independence) of mind, to rise superior to the reproach and opposition of so many of his professed Christian brethren, in behalf of the poor, oppressed and degraded slave...I trust that you will be encouraged to persevere, believing that God, who in all generations has been the God of the oppressed ...will strengthen you, and bless your efforts in the good cause for which you plead.[15]

Additionally, numerous Disciples congregations in Pennsylvania and Ohio, both White and African American, played roles in the Underground Railroad. Despite Alexander Campbell's declaration in *The Millennial Harbinger* to obey the Fugitive Slave Law, a Disciples congregation in Berrien, Michigan, resolved, among other things, "That choosing to 'obey God rather than man,' we will not assist the master in recapturing the servant that has escaped from his master, but will feed the poor panting fugitive, and point him to the North Star, abiding the penalty of the law."[16]

Amidst the ideological battle over slavery–and the tangible struggle for freedom for and by Black slaves–Christianity played a significant role in the daily lives of Black people, both free and enslaved. Black worship simply began to share the hope-filled story of the Gospel, sometimes using familiar worship styles still in the group's collective memory of worship in Africa. Kenneth Henry, in describing early Black Disciples worship, wrote:

> The call and response of the leader and people was a customary form of expression in African life, and easily dominated Black preaching style. It is still characteristic of many Black worship services today. None of these practices evolved as the result of a theological study. They were expressions of how a people had come to know and worship in their particular time and place. As long as we ignore the authenticity of this heritage and accept only the English and European traditions as legitimate, the Black prophets will remain unknown to Black and White Disciples. If we can relate to and be enriched by the Psalms of ancient Israel, surely the same is possible in regards to the African heritage in our midst.[17]

It is worth noting that even in the early days of Black Disciples worship, many were drawn to the tradition for the same reasons as White Disciples. The Campbells focused on making religion accessible and reasonable, and people felt compelled by a religion that was neither flashy nor overly emotional. On the flip side, Barton Stone drew many members who were moved precisely by the emotional connection to God that the Campbells frowned upon. For this reason, people of color within the Disciples showed the same diversity of worship styles as White Disciples. Many people of color worshiped in what might be considered a "sober" style relative to other traditions.

While controversy over slavery brewed along the eastern seaboard, the mistreatment of Native Americans did not garner as much attention. While Congregationalists and Methodists were involved in defending Native Americans, the early Disciples did not get involved with the well-being of indigenous Americans. Disciples ministers did not ignore Native Americans completely. Barton Stone wrote several sermons in Cherokee, and in 1833, Alexander Campbell wrote a critique of the Georgia business sector taking advantage of the Cherokee Nation. However, no follow-up was forthcoming by other Disciples at the time.[18] There is one compelling exception to this negligence—the story of James Trott. Scholar Garry Sparks writes that aside from Campbell's single article, James J. Trott—an ordained Methodist minister turned Disciples who married a Cherokee woman and worked with the Cherokee Nation in Georgia—appears the only notable exception to the denomination's apathy, if not contempt, toward the native peoples in the country at that time. After working with the Cherokee since the mid-1820s, Trott openly condemned Georgia's attempts to steal Native lands in the early 1830s. He wrote to Alexander Campbell, "My heart's desire and prayer to God is that the primitive gospel may be introduced, prevail, and triumph among this oppressed people."[19] For his outspokenness, state authorities arrested, chained, and eventually banished Trott from the region.[20] Regardless, Trott returned and continued to work with the Cherokees until their forced move to present-day Oklahoma—the Trail of Tears—in 1838.[21] He returned to them again in 1856 to work not just on converting members of that indigenous nation but also to work with them on social, political, and educational issues, interrupted briefly again only by the Civil War.[22] Unfortunately his "Christian Mission to the Cherokees" was never regularly supported by the Disciples. Trott noted that the richest Christians had "no sympathy for the Indians!"[23]

Members' identities were still in formation in the early days of the Disciples, so some today might excuse their lack of involvement with "political issues" such as slavery and the genocide of Native Americans. Almost from its founding, however, one "political" issue remained less than abstract for the founders of the Disciples. More than one scholar has said that we would read our history differently if we thought of ourselves not as a denomination founded by pioneers (like John "Raccoon" Smith and Walter Scott), but rather as a denomination founded by immigrants.

Geunhee Yu, Executive Pastor of Asian Ministries for the Christian Church (Disciples of Christ) is fond of pointing out that three of the four founders of the Christian Church (Disciples of Christ) were adult immigrants, much like the vast majority of North American Pacific and Asian Disciples (NAPAD) members today. He also noted that the early church in the Bible took into account the needs of immigrants as their Jerusalem-based movement took root by electing Greeks for all seven of their new leaders (Acts 6:1-7). He writes that it is fascinating

> [T]hat many (Western) frontier people in the 19th century were mostly (im)migrants seeking new homes, spiritual as well as physical. The church responded to their needs seriously by welcoming them, especially to 'the Table.' It is no wonder that the church grew like wildfire.[24]

Is it as immigrants and children of immigrants that the Disciples moved so quickly into the realm of mission work, desiring to share their good news throughout the world? Perhaps—and perhaps early Disciples were influenced by "the White Man's Burden," a common expression at the time coined by the British writer, Rudyard Kipling. It alluded to the notion that, as the superior race and culture, White people had an obligation to civilize others. This meant sharing the White religion of salvation and the White culture that was part of that salvation.

History is never as clear-cut as we would like it to be. White Disciples strived to shape the society around them. Likewise, the existing society shaped them. The same, in some ways, is true for Disciples of color. So while the second missionary the Disciples sent abroad was Alexander Cross, a Black man and a slave freed for the purpose of mission work, his race does not negate the influence of the White Man's Burden on his actions. The Hopkinsville Ky. Christian Church bought Cross, a great preacher, for the discounted rate of $530 (he was "worth" $1,500 but his master approved of his ministry and offered a lower price) so that he could go with his free wife and seven-year-old son to do mission work in Liberia. His commissioning service was held before a packed congregation including 200 African Americans in the balcony. He died in Liberia two months into his journey, as did his son. There is no indication as to what became of his wife. He was the movement's second missionary, the first having been sent to Jerusalem.

The Disciples' first foray into mission work happened during the era of slavery. Black members of mixed congregations continued to join the Disciples during this period, and Black Disciples continued to establish their own congregations (generally under White parent churches in slave states):

> By 1861 the African American membership in mixed congregations numbered about 5,500, and in separate congregations about 1,500. The mixed congregations were in Kansas, Kentucky, Mississippi, Missouri, North Carolina, Ohio, Pennsylvania, Tennessee, Texas, and Virginia. The separate congregations were in Georgia, Kentucky, North Carolina, and Tennessee.[25]

Notes

[1] To be fair, the founders' vision of the early church relied on the picture painted by the book of Acts that initially portrays a community where all is shared in common and people live in unity and Christian love. The majority of Paul's epistles (written before the book of Acts, and some before the gospels), however, were written to address fierce conflicts in the early church over everything from the role of circumcision among new Christians to Christ's divinity to who would be saved.

[2] Guin Stemmler, *A Mini History: The Christian Church (Disciples of Christ)* (St. Louis: Christian Board of Publication, 1974), 3.

[3] Ibid., 7.

[4] William K. Fox, Sr. "African Americans in the Movement," in *The Encyclopedia of the Stone-Campbell Movement,* ed. Douglas A. Foster, Paul M. Blowers, Anthony L Dunnavant, and D. Newell Williams (Grand Rapids, Mich.: William B. Eerdmans, 2004), 10–11.

[5] This date is contested, with contradictory records.

[6] William Harold McDonald, "Ripples: A History of the Midway Christian Church, Midway, Kentucky" (MDiv dissertation, Lexington Theological Seminary, 1985.)

[7] William K. Fox, Sr. "African Americans in the Movement," *Encyclopedia*, 11.

[8] Kenneth Henry, "Unknown Prophets: Black Disciple Ministry in Historical Perspective," *Discipliana* 46 (Spring 1986): 5.

[9] Secondary sources write about a past event–a history book for example. By contrast, primary sources are created at the with time of the event itself (a newspaper article from the day after John Kennedy was assassinated or the handwritten text of Abraham Lincoln's Gettysburg Address).

[10] R. Frederick West and William Garrett West, *Who Are The Christian Churches and What Do We Believe?* (published by the authors, 1954), 18.

[11] The Greek word *eschaton* here means "end times," a major aspect of some early Disciples' concerns as the year 1900 approached. A number of "Millennialists" who played prominent roles in the beginnings of the Disciples story faded from leadership after 1900. They were disappointed that 1900 came and went without an apocalyptic visit of some sort. Many eschaton-focused Christians avoided involvement in "political" issues, believing that Christ's second coming was so near that earthly issues would soon be resolved without their involvement.

[12] From a *Millennial Harbinger* article published in September 1851 as quoted by John H. Hull, "Underground Railroad Activity Among Western Pennsylvania Disciples," *Discipliana* 57, no. 1 (Spring 1997): 5.

[13] The term "restorationist movement" refers to the founders' desire to restore the first-century church in the present day, without the additions of either Catholicism or Protestants' then 300-year old Reformation.

[14] Hull, "Underground Railroad Activity," 7.

[15] Ibid.

[16] Ibid., 10.

[17] Kenneth Henry, "Unknown Prophets: Black Disciple Ministry in Historical Perspective," *Discipliana* (Spring 1986): 4.

[18]Garry Sparks, "The Relationship of the Christian Church (Disciples of Christ) to Native Americans," (unpublished paper, University of Chicago, 2002), 5.

[19]James J. Trott, "Letter to the Editor of the Millennium Harbinger," *The Millennium Harbinger* 3 (February 1832): 85. Quoted in David Edwin Harrell Jr, *Quest for Christian America, 1800–1865: A Social History of the Disciples of Christ*, vol. 1 (Tuscaloosa: University of Alabama Press, 2003), 210.

[20]Ibid., 209.

[21]Ibid., 210.

[22]Ibid., 211.

[23]James J. Trott, "Mission to the Cherokees," *The Gospel Advocate* (February 1856): 63–64. See also Sparks, 6, footnotes 12 through 15.

[24]Geunhee Yu, "At the Two Tables: Communion and Common," *Mid-Stream* 40, no. 3 (July, 2001).

[25]William K. Fox, Sr. "African Americans in the Movement," *Encyclopedia*, 11.

2

Westward Ho!

American Expansion, Mission, and People of Color—1865-1900

"We didn't cross the border; the border crossed us," joke some Chicanos[1] living in the Southwest. When the Guadalupe-Hidalgo Treaty of 1848 divided the United States and Mexico, many Hispanics already lived in what is now the United States, having lived there longer than the White settlers who moved into New Mexico, Arizona, and Texas. The prevalence in the 1800s of Spanish-speaking people in what is now the United States should come as little surprise; the first Christians to reach the Americas were Hispanic. Disciples' historian Daisy Machado points to the Spanish names of so many American cities including San Augustine, San Antonio, El Paso, and San Diego.[2] We tend to think of White American expansion into the Southwest as a frontier movement, much as we think of the Disciples as a frontier religion. However, just as our founders were mostly immigrants, we might also think of the White

Americans who came to the southwest as immigrants of a sort. Machado notes:

> The historical fact is that the frontier settlers of North America who moved westward in the nineteenth century were immigrants entering foreign soil. In the crossing of each river in the province of Coahuila y Texas–the Sabine, Trinity and Nueces rivers–these Euro-American settlers were for the most part illegally penetrating the Spanish empire of Nueva España. Their arrival into the Spanish province of Coahuila y Texas meant that these settlers were coming into contact with a people and a reality for which they were the foreigners, the invaders, the Other ... This was Nueva España and then Mexico populated by a borderlands people whose world view was not Euro-American, whose race, culture, and language were different but not inferior. Yet this distinctiveness was either outright rejected or subordinated to all that was North American.[3]

Machado also notes that as a nation we have told a story of frontiersmen moving into an empty or inferior land. As a result of this reinvention, "Lost is the crucial examination and recognition of the vitality of the borderlands itself as a place in which a new culture was shaped. By assuming that the Texas borderlands was a forgotten land, or that the borderlands was a place where the 'superior' displaced 'inferior,' the deeper levels of meaning that belong to borderlands history is neglected."[4] This background becomes important as we examine the ways Disciples related to Hispanics in Puerto Rico (an American colony since 1898) versus Hispanics in their own "native" land.

According to Machado, the Stone-Campbell Movement reached Texas as early as 1824 when it was still part of Mexico. However, outreach to Latinos and Latinas did not begin until the late 1800s. Mission work abroad was a clear goal of early

Disciples, making Mexico a natural mission front.[5] The Mexican Revolution (1810–1821) may have contributed to the Disciples' shift in mission and ministry, but Latinos and Latinas constituted a significant portion of the population in Texas, while Disciples focused on mission across the border. A certain notion of who was and who was not "American" might have contributed to Disciples' blind eye to Hispanics in the United States, no matter who was there first. As has been previously noted, the Disciples were the first denomination founded on American soil. As a result, the Movement was shaped by distinctly American values. How would a distinctly American movement deal with the collision of manifest destiny (the notion that White immigrants and migrants to America were destined by God to claim American land for themselves) and the White Man's Burden (the notion that because of their innate superiority, White Christians had an obligation to civilize and Christianize the rest of the "heathen" world)?

It seems that the Disciples' internalization of these potentially conflicting notions would thereby result in a somewhat inconsistent approach to ministry with Hispanics in America and abroad. This can be noted in one particular mission project within the United States, one of the first for Latinos other than an ill-fated colony in Mexico in 1871:

> The very scant and meager records that tell about Disciples work amongst Latinos point to San Antonio as the site for the first meeting. The year was 1888 and a Disciples Mexican mission was started with the hope that it might spread the Disciples movement into Mexico. From the start the idea was not really to open a church for the Mexicans of San Antonio, but to use this group to prepare for missionary work in Mexico itself. This early attempt at work with Mexican-Texans was described as 'weak and intermittent' and there is no further mention of it until 1899.[6]

Even a project within the United States during this time focused on witnessing to Mexicans.

Following Machado, Pablo Jiménez believes that two reasons motivated this limited approach to Hispanic mission work in the United States:

> First, the Stone-Campbell Movement was an American frontier phenomenon that shared many of the ideological presuppositions of its time. It was shaped, thus, by the manifest destiny ideology, the myth that the frontier land was a "wilderness" to be conquered and civilized, and "paradigms of difference in which the indigenous people were identified as inferior because of their race, religion and culture." Second, Hispanics were largely considered foreigners; they were not considered real "Americans." This presupposition allowed members of the Stone-Campbell Movement to overlook even the people of Mexican ancestry who had lived for several generations in Texas, Oklahoma, New Mexico, Arizona, and California.[7]

While Latinos in the United States were essentially ignored, mission work in Mexico and Puerto Rico continued apace because of the White Man's Burden.

Meanwhile on the East Coast (and increasingly in the Midwest and into Texas), Black Disciples with newfound freedom were striving for educational opportunities and spiritual sustenance. Disciples historian Kenneth Henry points out the radical shifts in the lives of African Americans with the introduction of the Thirteenth, Fourteenth, and Fifteenth Amendments and attaining freedom. Suddenly they could work for pay, could travel when and where they wanted to, could purchase their own land, and could stay together as families without the fear of someone splitting them up. However, soon enough these freedoms, though still existing in theory, were in many cases taken away from the African American community as federal troops left the South and white supremacy regained its prior place. Henry mentions the death in 1917 of his paternal grandfather who was shot as he rode his wagon home from paying his poll tax. Henry's maternal mulatto grandfather died never knowing his own father, although he had seen his mother frequently beaten by her slave master. "This is the context," writes Henry, "within which African Americans had to make sense of the fellowship of the church, empowerment of the Holy Spirit, the justice of God, theodicy and eschatology. From this background, my father, older brother, five uncles and myself have given collectively more than 350 years to the ministry of the Christian Church."[8]

The numbers of African American Disciples grew in the immediate aftermath of the Civil War. Henry observes that this trend toward urbanization left Disciples, whose stronghold was predominantly rural, with less capacity to respond to the changing needs of the African American community.[9] As during slavery, the practice of White churches helping African Americans establish their own congregations rather than offering full participating membership to Blacks in their churches continued after the Civil War. It is true that this help was often gladly accepted by African Americans, who were wary of becoming second-class church members in a religion that proclaimed neither "Jew nor Greek, neither slave nor free." (Gal. 3:28) However, it should be noted that this was not a period in which Blacks abandoned the multicultural church, as is sometimes asserted.

Black Disciples churches expanded rapidly during this period, particularly in the rural South. By 1876 there were African American congregations in Alabama, Georgia, Indiana, Kansas, Kentucky, Louisiana, Michigan, Mississippi, Missouri, North Carolina, Ohio, South Carolina, Tennessee, Texas, and Virginia. The total membership had increased to approximately 20,000.[10] Membership in 1900 of African American Disciples of Christ in the United States was approximately 56,300 in 535 churches, twenty-one states, and the federal territory.[11]

A distinctive strand of the Christian Church began to emerge during this era. The churches now known as "Assembly Churches" were founded in the early 1870s. These churches, which often still go by "Church of Christ, Disciples of Christ" to this day, emerged out of the sense of many free Blacks and a few White Disciples leaders that Black Disciples along the eastern seaboard should have their own churches with their own structures. The White Disciples Conventions would offer some financial support, but the Black churches would be largely self-governed. What emerged was a collection of churches organized by districts that came together for general assemblies. These churches' greatest strength lay in eastern North Carolina (as remains the case today). While some Black Disciples churches would develop a structure parallel to (and eventually merged with) the White Disciples, the Assembly Churches would continue in an independent fashion with worship shaped strongly by the Free Will Baptists, who influenced all Disciples in that region. [12] They emphasized foot washing as essential to communion and often celebrated communion quarterly. Their parallel but distinct growth as a Disciples movement would serve throughout the church's life as a reminder of the challenges to the movement's commitment to "unity in diversity" in the face of (and sometimes denial of) the massive barriers to unity in America. White Disciples would begin to lose touch with Assembly Churches in 1901.

During this period in the Christian Church a fierce theological battle raged over the need for a literal interpretation of the Bible. Likewise, Disciples of color who had been drawn to the movement for diverse reasons faced some of these same battles. One early Black Disciples leader who worked in strong partnership with White Disciples embraced the Christian Church because of the space it provided for rationalism as a part of faith:

In Mississippi, Elder Eleven Woods (Levin Wood) led in the establishment of new churches. He was an effective evangelist and able to enlist significant white support. Woods had come from Warren County. Through his own study of the Bible and through the influence of a white Kentucky businessman, William T. Withers, Woods, who had left the Baptist Church because the Baptists required an "experience" prior to conversion, welcomed the Movement's requirement of a straightforward confession of faith. When Woods evangelized in Grand Gulf, the only church, a Baptist church, accused him of heresy for preaching a "new gospel." Woods was arrested and tried in court, but the judge ruled in his favor, noting that Woods' gospel was scripturally genuine. Woods founded a church in Grand Gulf and several others from Vicksburg to Natchez.[13]

African American churches in the quarter century after Reconstruction concentrated on evangelism, conventions, and education.[14] Despite this, only three Disciples institutions of higher education for African Americans existed at the end of the nineteenth century–others had petered out due to lack of funds. These three educational institutions focused on trades, not academics. White Disciples did not invest enough resources in the education of African Americans. The Methodist and Congregationalist churches invested far more in Black higher education. This lack of investment by White Disciples in Black higher education would contribute in the beginning of the twentieth century to Black Disciples' sense that they needed to create an autonomous organization to guarantee that their community's needs would be met. (This will be discussed at greater length in chapter 5.) In the late 1800s, though, Black Disciples (like the larger Black American community) had no infrastructure on which to rely, depending on assistance from their White Disciples brothers and sisters to help them establish the means for their advancement. It was during this era that the Southern Christian Institute was established, whose history continued until it merged with Tougaloo College in the 1950s. According to Kenneth Henry:

> Through the end of this period, the pattern of racial segregation dominated to the growing discomfort of Black Disciples. In 1890, the Board of Negro Education and Evangelism became the chief brotherhood instrument for the planning and direction of Negro work. The American Christian Missionary Society, and later

the Christian Woman's Board of Missions, took over the support of negro work. Major policies concerning Negro work were being shaped by White Disciples, with almost no input from Black Disciples.[15]

Asians—specifically Chinese people—began entering the United States in the mid-1850s, particularly when the United States sought cheap labor to build the Transcontinental Railroad. According to Disciples leader Geunhee Yu, "the first Asians entered the United States at essentially the same time as the Disciples first National Convention in 1849 in Cincinnati. However, since the Disciples' growth followed the westward expansion, Disciples had little presence in the West at that time and little opportunity to interact with the Asian community located predominantly west of the Mississippi River. It was not until 1891 that The Christian Woman's Board of Missions (CWBM) opened a mission among the Chinese in Portland, Oregon, and it grew so explosively that a Chinese minister (Jeu Hawk) was called to lead the work in 1892." [16] One historical challenge this mission faced was the Chinese Exclusion Act, enacted in 1882, banning any further immigration from China. This law made the continuation of such a ministry next-to-impossible unless the Disciples engaged in advocating for immigrants' rights, something very few churches did at the time. Regardless of this challenge, David Wetzel, a Portland pastor, shared his dream of developing a Chinese mission in March 1889. His dream became a reality on January 9, 1891:

> [A]nd by January 27, forty-five pupils were enrolled. The first meeting place was a large rented storeroom in which a day school was conducted as well as Sunday afternoon services. It was difficult to secure a suitable meeting place in those days, on account of the prejudice against the Chinese…In March, 1891, seven converts were baptized, among them Moy Ham who served as interpreter until he returned to China. For a short time after this, active work at the mission was suspended on

account of lack of workers and money, but those who had been baptized remained faithful to the cause and furnished the nucleus of the organized work later."[17]

It was restarted with the recruitment of Jeu Hawk, a Chinese man described in the following heroic terms (missionaries were often depicted in dramatic fashion in publicity materials in the early 1900s) by the United Christian Missionary Society:

A young Chinese left his father's house in China, forty miles from Canton, at the age of fifteen to come with his uncle to America where they were led to believe gold was picked up on the streets. When they landed at the "Golden Gate" in San Francisco not one word of English could they speak. After a few months they journeyed to St. Louis where they settled to work... Jeu Hawk—or Hawk Jeu, Hawk meaning learned—was sent to Sunday School in order that he might learn the English language. Through the teaching heard there he became a Christian and longing to preach to his own people in China it was arranged for him to enter Drake University at Des Moines, Iowa. He was the first foreigner to enter that school ... His uncle and father, both bitter enemies of Christianity, did everything to hinder him. One year when young Jeu was ready to return to Des Moines, his father took to his bed and refused to eat or drink if his son left him. Rather than bring the cause of Christ into disrepute among Chinese people by such unfilial action he stayed but all that year he would snatch moments from sleep and work to study his bible...And the next year he returned to college though his father disinherited him. A reconciliation was later effected ... In 1892 the Christian Woman's Board of Missions asked him to take charge of the newly opened mission among the Chinese in Portland, Oregon. Before taking up this new position he studied the methods used in conducting city missions elsewhere.

Within a short time his work began to show results of his earnest, forceful and tireless efforts.[18]

A remarkable detail about this early missionary was that "Jeu Hawk decided if he were to heal souls he ought also to be able to heal the bodies of his people, hence he studied medicine and graduated from the Portland Medical College ... Jeu Hawk was active in an effort to bring all the Chinese missions in Portland into a united action for the help of his people, and succeeded in having the first union meeting in February, 1894."[19] Two months later he helped host another meeting in the heart of Chinatown, as this would be closer to the people.[20] In 1900 Jeu Hawk and his wife returned to China.

Our denomination was founded during the contentious era of slavery, but even after the resolution of the issue of slavery with the end of the Civil War, American expansion into the West was viewed as a largely undebated "good." Often referred to as "manifest destiny," the notion that White Americans had a God-given right to claim American land west of the thirteen original colonies was virtually uncontested. In a few isolated instances, Methodists and Congregationalists stood in opposition to the displacement and even genocide of Native American tribes.

The Disciples, however, had rooted their identity in notions of pioneering and rugged individualism. These ideas played an important role in the way Disciples "do" church even today, evidenced by the autonomy that individual congregations enjoy within our denomination (while in covenant with regional and general church structures). The pioneering spirit of the Disciples might even have something to do with our current commitment to "1,000 new churches in 1,000 different ways" and our willingness to try new forms of church that allow for creativity and diversity. However, part of the pioneering spirit of White America in the late 1800s involved manifest destiny. As a tradition shaped by its Anglo-American context, Disciples capitalized on westward expansion without considering the well-being of the people into whose land they expanded. A primary example is the Disciples' rapid expansion into Oklahoma using the government's land grab strategy at the time to establish new churches in the territory while remaining silent about or perhaps blind to the displacement of the land's first inhabitants. The Disciples were not unique, as virtually no churches spoke out on this issue. However, the Disciples capitalized on this expansion movement in Oklahoma in palpable ways:

> Due to the land giveaway, rural Oklahoma became populated in an incredibly short period of time. There was a dwelling on almost every quarter-section, four families in each square mile. They were mostly young people in their 20s or 30s. The 1907 Disciples Year Book (the year Oklahoma became a state) reported that Oklahoma Disciples had about 200 churches. Listed were 286 preachers, including four women.[21]

Notes

[1] *Chicano* is a self-identifying term used by some people of Mexican descent living in the United States. When discussing the broader community of people from Cuba, Mexico, Central America and Puerto Rico, this book will alternately use "Latino/a" and "Hispanic." Although Latino and Latina is preferred by some authors (since most Latinos have little direct connection to the Spanish who conquered/colonized their native lands), the term Hispanic (which generally includes all Spanish-speaking people) continues to be the term used in official Disciples contexts at the General and Regional manifestations, such as the Central Pastoral Office for Hispanic Ministries in Indianapolis and the denomination's Hispanic Bilingual Fellowship.

[2] Samuel Pagán, "Hispanics and the Church," *The Disciple* (September 1990): 28.

[3] Daisy Machado, "From Ango-American [sic] Traditions to a Multicultural World," *Discipliana* 57 (Summer 1997), 52.

[4] Ibid., 51.

[5] Daisy L. Machado, *Of Borders and Margins: Hispanic Disciples in Texas, 1888–1945* (Oxford: Oxford University Press, 2003), 83–84.

[6] Carter E. Boren, *Religion on the Texas Frontier* (San Antonio: The Naylor Co., 1968), 292, as cited in Machado, *Discipliana* article, 53.

[7] Pablo A. Jiménez, "Hispanics in the Movement," in *The Encyclopedia of the Stone-Campbell Movement*, ed. Douglas A. Foster, Paul M. Blowers, Anthony L Dunnavant, and D. Newell Williams (Grand Rapids, Mich.: William B. Eerdmans, 2004), 395.

[8]Kenneth Henry, "Unknown Prophets: Black Disciple Ministry in Historical Perspective," *Discipliana* 46 (Spring 1986): 108.

[9]Ibid., 108.

[10]William K. Fox Sr., "African Americans in the Movement," in *Encyclopedia,* 12.

[11]Ibid., 13.

[12]William Joseph Barber, *Disciples Assemblies of Eastern North Carolina* (St. Louis: The Bethany Press, 1966), 33–38.

[13]Fox, "African Americans in the Movement," 11–12.

[14]Ibid., 12.

[15]Kenneth Henry, "Unknown Prophets: Black Disciple Ministry in Historical Perspective," *Discipliana* 46 (Spring 1986): 5–6.

[16]Geunhee Yu, "Asian American Disciples," *Encyclopedia,* 1.

[17]W. F. Turner, "The Portland Christian Mission," *World Call* (May 1923): 20.

[18]"Jeu Hawk," *United Christian Missionary Society Biography Set,* Series 1, Leaflet 9, 1933.

[19]Ibid.

[20]W. F. Turner, "Portland Christian Mission," 20.

[21]Eulis H. Hill, "The horse race that established Disciples in O-O-OKLAHOMA!" *The Disciple* (September 1993): 24.

3

What Is Mission?
1900-1925

"The Treaty of Paris was signed on December 10, 1898. By April, Lutherans, Episcopalians, Presbyterians, Methodists, Baptists, Congregationalists, United Brethren, and Disciples of Christ were permanently on the field [in Puerto Rico]. Some of these bodies were actually at work before the signing of the formal treaty and almost all had sent explorers to study the field before the event."

Dr. C. Manly Morton[1]

Disciples had largely turned a blind eye to indigenous Americans in their pursuit of ministry to White settlers. Likewise, they had chosen to invest little energy in ministering to and with Mexicans and Tejanos in the Southwest, even though White Disciples ministries were beginning to grow in the same area. However, as soon as the doors were open to mission work in Puerto Rico, the Disciples were one of the first groups to respond. Puerto Ricans would fast become one of the Disciples' most significant racial-ethnic groups, making up well over two-thirds of the Latino community within the Disciples, with Mexicans, Latin Americans and Chicanos making up a much smaller portion.

It is true that Disciples had very quickly decided to claim mission work as a primary focus of their identity. However, the definition of mission work was still being developed and would continue to evolve over the course of its history. For this reason, ministry within U. S. borders sometimes had different emphases than mission work abroad, where the "mission" was clearer–to introduce Christianity (and the White culture that was assumed to be a part of that Christianity), thereby saving non-Christians. The ways in which culture and religion got combined are well exemplified in a quote from recent Disciples history. Byron Spice served in the denomination's Division of Homeland Ministries in the 1960s with a particular focus on ministry in the Hispanic community. In a book he wrote about Disciples' history in that area, he described the first successful Disciples Hispanic church in Texas and raised an interesting question for contemporary readers:

> In the spring of 1899, George B. Ramshaw, who was secretary of the American Christian Missionary Society at the time, learned of a group of Mexicans in San Antonio who were searching for greater religious liberty than they had been accustomed to in the Catholic church. He visited their meetings and preached a series of revival sermons through an interpreter. As a result he baptized a number of persons and with them as a nucleus organized a Mexican Christian Church in San Antonio. The first pastor was a man named Y. Quintero.
>
> On June 1, 1899, the American Christian Missionary Society approved the first appropriation to a Spanish-language Christian Church. This was the beginning. What has been accomplished since then? How successful have we been in sharing our faith with Spanish-speaking people?[2]

In a country that was already more diverse than most White Americans acknowledged, railroad construction in the West had made America even more diverse. Laborers came from China (and then Japan to work in the fields to meet labor shortages during the Gold Rush in California). Mission work abroad was fairly clear, but how would we missionize and civilize our own people? Who were our own people? Clearly "our" people did not include those who spoke Spanish, according to Spice. In the first quarter of the twentieth century, these questions would challenge Disciples' domestic ministries in significant ways, especially when free Blacks faced increasing backlash after Reconstruction. Were they objects of mission in the United States, charity cases or independent Christians with their own churches? Were they part of "our faith"?

Mexican pastors, presumably trained in Mexican schools by Disciples missionaries, ran all the first Latino Disciples churches in the United States. This speaks to the reality, notes Daisy Machado, that White Texan Disciples considered Mexican Texans (sometimes called Tejanos) as "others," foreign, and not worth training within Texas itself. This also led to a lack of indigenously-trained leadership within the Mexican American population in Texas, with long-term ramifications for that community.[3] Finding ministers for these congregations fell under the auspices of the Christian Woman's Board of Missions, and a Disciples missionary from Mexico supervised them.

The church in San Antonio that Byron Spice wrote about was seemingly disbanded in 1905 without any clear explanation. The next recorded effort to establish a Spanish-speaking church in the area was to reestablish the previous church in 1908. This resulted in what is now one of the denomination's five "home mission sites," the Inman Center.[4] The church was started with a visit from S. Guy Inman and Mexican pastor Felipe Jiménez.

By 1916 Hispanic Disciples had created the "State Mexican S.S. Convention," made up of seven congregations that would form and then disband at times during the ensuing years.[5] In 1913 the Mexican Christian Institute (now the Inman Center) was established in San Antonio to respond to the needs of the Mexican-Texan community. The articulated purpose was:

> To bring this large group of Mexican people–ignorant and superstitious and with a low standard of morals–to a knowledge of Christ … Why should we seek to bring Christ to the Spanish-speaking people in the United States? We are not only under obligation to our Lord to make Christians of these, people, but we also have a patriotic obligation to make of them good citizens of our fair nation.[6]

Countless articles from the time cited the struggles of Latino pastors to make ends meet and to address the needs of their congregations; their pleas for financial assistance for basic needs like meeting space, Spanish-language materials and salary for the pastors, appear by-and-large to have remained unmet. Machado suggests this stemmed from the ambivalence reflected in comments such as those above: how does one motivate financial assistance for a people considered un-American and possibly unchangeably so?

Inman Center remains significant in the life of the church. A document from 1964 states: "Established in 1913 in an underdeveloped area housing more than 22,000 Mexicans, the [Inman] Center has been instrumental in encouraging great improvement in the community."[7] Even in 1964, this framing of the Center's purpose indicates a certain "missionary mindset" among Disciples at the time. Machado asserts that the center provided "Texas Disciples a way to assume the role of benevolent giant as opposed to that of humble servant. Given the many layers of manifest destiny ideology so prevalent during this time, the important task of 'civilizing and Christianizing' inferior 'strangers' was a role the Disciples understood."[8]

In addition to the inconsistent relationship of the White Disciples church to Mexican American Disciples (and potential Disciples), the denomination had a strong and distinct relationship with the Puerto Rican church. Puerto Rico became a territory in 1898, and by 1899, the first Disciples missionaries were already in Puerto Rico.[9] The rapid response of White missionaries in Puerto Rico contrasted with the relative indifference White Disciples took toward Tejanos might speak to the sense of White Disciples at the time that Latinos were un-American and thus objects of, rather than partners in, mission. Churches established in Puerto Rico led to strong Puerto Rican Disciples churches on the mainland, generally established by Puerto Rican immigrants and led by ministers trained at Evangelical Seminary of Puerto Rico, including the flagship La Hermosa Christian Church founded in New York in 1943.[10]

White Disciples struggled to keep Latino mission churches in Texas viable over the next twenty years. An excerpt from an article in the November 1920 World Call might give some insight into why that was the case:

Many of [the Mexicans and Spanish-Americans in the United States] are in a very destitute condition, live in crowded, unsanitary quarters and become ready victims of disease and crime. Large numbers are illiterate; the majority of them do not speak English; many are positively un-American.[11]

The cultural assumptions of our frontier tradition were next-to-impossible to transcend, even for the sake of the missionary efforts so central to our founding under the influence of immigrant Walter Scott. This slowed the growth of the Christian Church (Disciples of Christ) in the Southwest at the time, even relative to other Protestant denominations.

The Chinese mission in Portland, Oregon was judged so successful that in 1907 the Christian Woman's Board of Missions (CWBM) started the Chinese Christian Institute in San Francisco, an endeavor that survived until 1923. [12] The San Francisco Mission was established during the strongest days of the Portland mission, but the effects of the Chinese Exclusion Act were just around the corner:

The work of this [Portland Chinese] mission reached high tide during the days of Louis Hugh [1900–1910], but it has since encountered peculiar difficulties. First, came the Chinese exclusion law causing a decline in Chinese immigration, a decrease in Chinese population and frequent changes of residence from city to city, all of which affected the strength and continuity of the work. Second, the mission has had periods without native Chinese leadership."[13]

Finally the supporters of the Portland Chinese mission had to face demographic realities. In a letter to the Churches of Christ in Portland, Oregon, the United Christian Missionary Society's local advisory board recommended that the mission be closed effective February 1924, with the remaining members finding church homes among the American churches in the area.

The Chinese Exclusion Act of 1880 left a significant labor gap that Japanese people were ready and able to fill; conditions in Japan were poor, and relations between Japan and the United States were good, so that when Chinese people were prohibited from immigrating to the United States, Japanese immigrants met the labor demands of the rapidly-expanding American West. In addition to those laborers, a number of students from Japan studied in California in those years. This in part explains the investment of the Disciples into the Japanese Christian Institute in Berkeley, California in 1907. The story of the Japanese Christian Institute in Berkeley will be told in greater detail in chapter 6, since its most significant changes occurred during the late 1920s. The next section will also tell the greater story of the Japanese Christian Institute/Church in Los Angeles, but an incredibly progressive pamphlet distributed by the Division of Homeland Ministries during the 1930s describes the Los Angeles church's beginnings in these dramatic terms:

Because they could stand long hours in the broiling sun, because they could make the desert bloom like a rose, the Japanese were brought to this country by selfish white men. With large promises they began to import great numbers of these workers who later transformed thousands of acres of southern California into beautiful gardens.

But the greed of the white man soon desired to possess the fruit of the labor of the Japanese. They became ostracized and hated. They were good enough to do the work but not good enough to find a place to live.

In 1908 the minister of Broadway Christian Church in Los Angeles saw the great need and with the help of two or three interested persons he opened a night school to teach English and the requirements of citizenship to the Japanese young men. They soon recognized the need of a Christian home also for Japanese young men and a boarding home was established. The Christian Woman's Board of Missions took over the responsibility for the support of the Japanese work later in 1908."[14]

According to Disciples historian William Fox, many Black Disciples saw evangelism and education of Blacks as inextricably linked, a connection the Christian Woman's Board of Missions agreed with:

To this end, beginning in 1900 the Board provided administrative oversight of fifteen schools founded mainly by black leaders, primarily to prepare African Americans to become teachers or ministers. Despite good intentions, most schools failed after less than a decade of existence.[15]

Southern Christian Institute (SCI) in Edwards, Mississippi, a mission school headed successively by Joel Baer Lehman (1890–1922) and John Cornelius Long (1925–54), had the longest term of success. In a period when Mississippi spent less than a fifth as much per child on the education of blacks as on whites, SCI educated hundreds of African Americans at the elementary and secondary levels, as well as smaller numbers at the college level. In 1954, when a more adequate system of public education had become available to blacks in Mississippi, the school, which by then had become a junior college, was merged into Tougaloo College.[16]

SCI had its own publication, *The Gospel Plea,* with editorialists like J. B. Lehman. In explaining the need for a school like SCI, one editorial noted: "If the negro race is to be introduced into our industrial and business world without the development of his conscience and religious instincts, then we will have only that many more grafters and cunning politicians to live as parasites on honest industry. We already have too many white grafters and politicians and we need not add to the list from elsewhere."[17] SCI sought to make itself the central location for Black Disciples ministry, although its leadership and teachers were White.

Strong as SCI might have been (it was sometimes referred to by Black Disciples as "Our Tuskeegee," since it focused primarily on trade education in its early days), the fact remained, that White Disciples invested relatively little in higher education for Blacks, choosing instead to focus on cultivating skills in basic trades.[18]

The story of A.J. Hurdle illustrates this gap between articulated goal and application. A freed Black slave and Disciples minister, Hurdle strongly advocated for the Disciples to establish a Black Disciples college in Texas. When he met with fierce resistance from the White leadership, he raised funds outside of official Disciples channels and alienated a number of White Disciples who wanted him to wait for them to organize. Northeast Texas Christian Theological and Industrial College opened in 1912 thanks to the fundraising efforts of A.J. Hurdle and others, although a fire a few decades later ended its service. Interestingly, when Hurdle requested aid in his old age from the Pension Fund, the much-beloved president of the Southern Christian Institute, J.B. Lehman suggested Hurdle was too much of a troublemaker to warrant benefits from the denomination.

Lehman used his influence to instate a pension for Hurdle several years later, commenting to the pension fund, "I have yours [letter] of the 5th in reference to A. J. Hurdle of Texas. You wrote me once before about him and I did not then recommend [sic] his case. Some twenty years ago he led a split in Texas called the North East. He did all in his power to keep his people from cooperating with the white people and he made us a world of trouble. But now he is old and his sons are cooperating nicely with all our work and I believe it would be the part of wisdom to help him. He himself is very reasonable now. I advise giving him $10 per month."[19]

The difficulties Hurdle faced in mobilizing support for higher education for Black Disciples points to one of the main reasons Black Disciples would soon feel forced to create a separate, parallel structure for Black Disciples Churches in 1917. The leader in this movement was the enterprising and charismatic Preston Taylor.

"Preston Taylor made the good confession one Sunday morning, was baptized in the afternoon and preached his first sermon that same night. This occurred in a small meeting of servants held in the kitchen of a great house that stood at the corner of 4th and Walnut Streets, Louisville, Kentucky."[20] Among his many efforts on behalf of the Brotherhood (as the Stone-Campbell Movement often was called then), Taylor raised funds for what became the Louisville Bible College and also organized the Lea Avenue Church in Nashville, which he pastored for forty years. He established an undertaking business, built a factory to make his own caskets, and opened both Greenwood Cemetery and the amusement park called Greenwood Park in Nashville. As director and chair of the executive committee for Citizens Savings Bank and Trust Company, he helped the Masons build their Old Folks' Home and Orphanage, Masonic Temple, as well as the Odd Fellows. He served as first president of the National Christian Missionary Convention for the fourteen years until his death, and he bequeathed all his investments to the Convention. "His estate owns and operates the most beautiful park and cemetery of his race, consisting of 150 acres. It is reported he was recently offered $1,000 per acre for it. He replied, 'No, money will not buy it. I want it to always belong to my people.'"[21]

The National Christian Missionary Convention (NCMC) that Taylor established and led until his death emerged because of growing concerns among Black Disciples that they were neither funded sufficiently nor given enough autonomy in their ministry as part of the predominantly white institutional structures of the Christian Church. In writing on the formation of the NCMC, Kenneth Henry notes, "Self determination was the call of the Black prophets, with a stern challenge to their constituency for responsible stewardship of the resources that belonged to God."[22] Disciples Historian Robert L. Jordan stated that the purpose of the Convention, organized on August 9, 1917, was "to create a medium of self-expression and cooperative endeavor for development of our churches that our best contribution may be made to our posterity and to the world."[23]

It is essential to understand that the purpose of the NCMC was not to function as a separatist movement (Marcus Garvey's Black Separatism had little resonance within a group that had chosen to function as a small minority in a predominantly White church). During his inaugural address at the first NCMC in 1917, Preston Taylor stated that "The Disciples of Christ, strange as it may seem, need the colored people, if for no other reasons, as the acid test of Christian orthodoxy and willingness to follow the Christ all of the way in His program of human redemption. For if the white brother can include in his religious theory and practice the colored people as real brothers he will have avoided the heresy of all heresies."[24] Black Disciples did not want to leave the Disciples. Despite feeling that they were not a significant priority for White Disciples, the NCMC was established as a way to remain in relationship with White Disciples as equals instead of simply as objects of occasional mission and charity.

Kenneth Henry summarizes Preston Taylor's inaugural address concisely here (the entirety of this historic document, available in the online appendix, should be added to the Disciples canon along with Barton Stone's Last Will and Testament of the Springfield Presbytery and the Declaration and Address by Thomas Campbell):

> From the address delivered by Preston Taylor, the most prominent leader in the [National Christian Missionary Convention], and the views expressed by many at the historic meeting on August 5–9, 1917 in Nashville, Tennessee, these pushing and pulling forces may be characterized in the following way:
>
> Black Disciples were pushed in the direction of forming the convention by a general attitude of many Whites that the Negro was a ward, pet, or second class human being, not a full equal partner in the family of Disciples.
>
> The question of race was addressed in moving speeches at the General Convention occasionally, but little application was made to how Blacks were treated in terms of accommodations at the meetings, or even as they traveled in the interest of the church program.
>
> A lack of communication and misunderstanding of how Blacks were served by the agencies of the church was another pushing force.
>
> The formation of the convention was not just a negative reaction, but also an affirmation of basic beliefs that may be regarded as pulling forces.
>
> Black Disciples were seeking a mechanism for discussion and decision-making about their own needs. Nurturing the faith, strengthening the witness among Black Americans needed the regular and systematic input of Black Disciples.
>
> Recognizing immediately their need for prepared leadership, they affirmed a desire for a school of higher education, particularly for ministerial training. Preston Taylor charged that there was no first-rate, four-year college for Negroes in 1917. As recently as 1940, *The*

Christian Plea reported that while there were twenty-one Disciples-related colleges for Whites to study for the ministry, only Drake, Eureka, and Butler would accept Negroes. Chapman was later added to this list.

The need for a medium of communication was identified for continued nurture of Black church life.[25]

In 1918, the year after the National Convention was established, the Disciples began connecting with Native Americans who were aware of the Disciples. The Yakima Mission, the Disciples' only sustained official work with Native Americans, resulted in 1919. Its story is a complex one that will be spun out in greater detail in later chapters.[26] Interestingly, though, in the same year that Disciples began to minister to (not yet with) Native Americans (1919), the presence of Mexicans in Texas was referred to as the "Mexican Problem" in Disciples newspapers.[27] Pablo Jimenéz writes: "This reaction was no doubt due to the increased migration of Mexicans who, fleeing the revolution, had moved into the southwest borderlands of the United States. The issue is, How can a church minister effectively to a population that is considered foreign, inferior, and transitory?"[28] The question is particularly poignant when that population consists of one's own countrymen.

In 1920, the denomination issued the following statement about those fellow citizens:

> The study of missionary conditions and needs in the Southwest among the Mexicans who have come into the United States, just completed and reported to the Home Missions Council by Jay S. Stowell, who undertook the work under the direction of the Interchurch World Movement, shows that there are approximately 1,500,000 Mexicans and Spanish-Americans in the United States, with an increase which has been very great during the war and the troublous times in Mexico ... Many of these people are in a very destitute condition, live in crowded, unsanitary quarters

and become ready victims of disease and crime. Large numbers of them are illiterate; the majority of them do not speak English; many are positively anti-American.[29]

It is not surprising, given White Disciples' attitudes towards Latinos that the State Mexican S.S. Convention, first recorded in 1916, shows records of continuation only until 1922, picking up again in 1944. There were seven affiliated with plans for expansion.[30]

That said, ministry in the Latino community did grow between 1904 and 1927 in Texas.

In this twenty-three year period eleven new churches were started, four of which were initiated by Latinos themselves. [The Robstown mission started in 1912, with ACMS foreseeing it as continuing indefinitely as a mission because of its membership of seasonal and transient laborers; however it continues today as the self-supporting Iglesia Cristiana Bet-El. A similar mission in Lockhart in 1913 eventually closed.] There is then an eighteen-year gap between the last church founded in 1927 in McAllen and the next new Latino church started in 1945 in Brownsville.[31]

Notes

[1]Dr. C. Manly Morton, *Kingdom Building in Puerto Rico* (n.p., 1949), 13, as quoted by Pablo Cotto in *The Church's Problem in Relation to Puerto Rican Migration into New York City* (unpublished dissertation, Eastern Baptist Theological Seminary, Philadelphia, April 1950), 43.

[2]Byron Spice, *Discípulos Americanos: Sixty-five Years of Christian Churches' Ministry to Spanish Speaking Persons,* (Indianapolis: UCMS, Department of World Outreach Education, 1964), 45.

[3]Daisy L. Machado, *Of Borders and Margins: Hispanic Disciples in Texas, 1888–1945* (Oxford: Oxford University Press, 2003), 92.

[4]Daisy Machado, "From Ango-American [sic] Traditions to a Multicultural World," *Discipliana* 57 (Summer 1997), 54.

[5]Pablo A. Jiménez, "Hispanics in the Movement," in *The Encyclopedia of the Stone-Campbell Movement,* ed. Douglas A. Foster, Paul M. Blowers, Anthony

L Dunnavant, and D. Newell Williams (Grand Rapids, Mich.: William B. Eerdmans, 2004), 396.

⁶Machado, *Of Borders and Margins,* 97–98.

⁷UCMS biography of E.G. Luna (February 1964.)

⁸Machado, *Of Borders and Margins,* 97.

⁹Jiménez, "Hispanics in the Movement," 396.

¹⁰As in Texas, little effort was made to train Puerto Rican ministers in the United States. The long-range impact of this may be seen in the proposal at the 2003 General Assembly to facilitate the immigration of Disciples ministers from Latin America due to the lack of trained pastors on the mainland for the Latino community.

¹¹Machado, *Of Borders and Margins,* 96.

¹²According to Geunhee Yu, "Asian American Disciples," it was not until sixty-seven years later (1990) that the Disciples Chinese ministry was rekindled by a local congregation, First Christian Church in Alhambra, California. Disciples Chinese ministries are currently expanding with a staff person focusing one-third time on national Chinese ministries.

¹³W. F. Turner, "The Portland Christian Mission," *World Call* (May 1923): 21.

¹⁴Japanese Christian Institute pamphlets published by Home Missions Pioneering in 1934. From biographical files at Disciples Historical Society.

¹⁵William K. Fox Sr., "African Americans in the Movement," in *Encyclopedia,* 13.

¹⁶Ibid.

¹⁷Edwards, "Helpful to All," *The Gospel Plea* 18 (January 4, 1913): 1. For a fascinating primary source indicating how White Disciples leaders described the function of SCI, see the 1922 article "The Race Problem Solved!" from *World Call.*

¹⁸For people familiar with debates at the turn of the twentieth century the tension between these two options will not be surprising. The difference is that existing documents indicate that Black Disciples favored access to higher education whereas White Disciples felt Blacks needed only the more basic education opportunities, disallowing Black Disciples to make their own decisions on the matter.

¹⁹JB. Lehman to F. E. Smith, September, 10, 1931, in A.J. Hurdle Bio file, Disciples Historical Society, Nashville, Tennessee.

²⁰Grant K. Lewis, "Preston Taylor Joins the Larger Convention: An Appreciation of a Negro Leader," *World Call* (June 1931): 23.

²¹Ibid., 24.

²²Kenneth Henry, "Unknown Prophets: Black Disciple Ministry in Historical Perspective," *Discipliana* 46 (Spring 1986):5–6.

²³Cited in Fox, "African Americans in the Movement," 14.

²⁴Cited in Kenneth Henry, "The Black Disciples Heritage: Authentic, Vital, and Enduring," *Discipliana* 34 (Summer 1976): 15.

[25]Ibid., 110.

[26]Garry Sparks, "The Relationship of the Christian Church (Disciples of Christ) to Native Americans," (unpublished paper, University of Chicago, 2002), 8. One of the complexities of the mission's story involves its name, as well as the Anglo name for the Native Americans. Historically, the government referred to the federated tribe of many smaller Native American tribes as Yakima, but then changed it to Yakama in the 1990s in keeping with how the Native Americans referred to themselves. The name of the mission was also changed to Yakama, but the spellings in this history reflect whatever spelling was in use at the time being discussed.

[27]Machado, *Of Borders and Margins*.

[28]Jiménez, "Hispanics in the Movement," 396.

[29]"Mexicans in the United States," *World Call* (November 1920): 48.

[30]David Vargas, "A Historical Background of the National Hispanic and Bilingual Fellowship," *Discipliana* 46 (Fall 1986): 38.

[31]Machado, *Discipliana* article, 54.

4

Us, Them, and Brotherhood
1925–World War II

Ben Watson wrote about second-generation Asian Americans in a 1926 *World Call* article, "A 'Yellow Peril' or 'Golden Opportunity'?" observing:

These youth not only have the handicap of criticism from older ones, but also the very distinct handicap, and that is a mild word, of having parents who are not American citizens, and who according to law never can be citizens. So a barrier is fixed, fixed by law … The oriental problem in America is a problem of the American-born. Being citizens by right of birth they long to be treated as such, yet they are not treated as Americans. Isolated, segregated, lonely and hurt, they are a people without a country. This is not right. It is not American. Neither is it Christian! … Right bravely have they been struggling against these handicaps. The Christian groups have tried to live down the hurt and forget the humiliation which they frequently experience—too often at the hands of Americans whose names are on some church roll, but who seem to have missed the spirit of Christ. These friends from across the Pacific do not ask for special concessions; they scorn condescension. All they ask is justice and a fair deal; to be given credit only on merit, in this land which promises "liberty and justice for all." How loudly we shout that phrase and how little we practice it![1]

In the years between World Wars I and II, the United States continued its internal conflict between a need for labor that outpaced its "native" (White) supply and its inclination against embracing "foreigners," (including non-Whites who were born in the United States and were legally citizens) as equals. Disciples ministry to and with Japanese Christians up until the outbreak of World War II was generally a healthy and fairly progressive ministry, allowing for a significant amount of self-governance and autonomy for the pastors of the Disciples' four Japanese-language congregations. The most famous of these was the Japanese Christian Institute in Los Angeles (which would eventually become the two churches of the West Adams Christian Church and All Peoples Christian Center—more on that history in the next chapter). Another was a Japanese church in Berkeley, California, whose history with the denomination began as far back as 1907. At this time, the CWBM's superintendent of Oriental Missions noted in a report: "The Japanese night school held in the Christian Church is in a flourishing condition." Thirty Japanese, largely university students, gathered to study English literature, begin a YMCA, and worship together.[2] CWBM gave them twenty-five dollars per month toward rent of a three-room space.

The new ministry to Japanese Americans was highlighted in *World Call*:

The University Christian Church in this city where Charles M. Watson is serving as a most efficient pastor, has been cooperating with the Japanese Church which

is supported by the United Christian Missionary
Society. Mr. Watson, who stands on the basis that
the race problem must be solved by the good will
and service of the local church toward other races,
encourages the members of his church to live up to the
spirit of universal brotherhood....

Since there are many American-born Japanese in
Berkeley we must have English service for them for
they must be assimilated into the spirit of America to
be fitted for citizenship, knowing that the principles of
Jesus are the foundation of American ideals....

Sometimes the young people of the two churches
[UCCB and Japanese Church] have a joint social
gathering to cultivate good fellowship with each other.
Not only so, the University Christian Church organized
a committee on Japanese work to cooperate with us
in every way possible. In this way we are getting the
deepest conviction that Christians can and must end
race wrongs and injustice by the Golden Rule. The
work of cooperation has been touching many hearts,
not only in our own churches, but the hearts of people
in other churches in the community ... Jesus came to
be the Savior of the world and to establish the Kingdom
of God on earth. Christianity is the vital force which
can solve the problems of race prejudice and secure
the cooperation of every race in bringing peace and
unity to the world. The little work of cooperation
in Berkeley will be a torch to lighten up one step in
reaching the solution of the great problem at present
in the world.[3]

The language about assimilation and citizenship in the
article—"for they must be assimilated into the spirit of America
to be fitted for citizenship, knowing that the principles of Jesus
are the foundation of American ideals"—was fairly common
for proponents of such ministries at the time. Many Japanese

Americans later used this same language to justify their work in the face of accusations that teaching Japanese to the youth was a sign of their disloyalty to the United States.

This was a complicated time for the Christian Church (Disciples of Christ) to invest itself in ministry to Japanese Americans. The Japanese had been encouraged to immigrate to meet farm labor shortages in California, particularly after the limiting of Chinese immigration in the late 1800s. However, attitudes about the presence of Japanese and Japanese Americans changed. In 1913 the California Alien Land Law banned the lease of land for farming to Japanese people, and this law was upheld by the Supreme Court in 1923. In 1924 (the same year as the above article from *World Call*), the Alien Immigration Act became law, banning the immigration of any people ineligible for citizenship (as East Asians and South Asians had all previously been banned from, with a series of Supreme Court decisions in the first quarter of the twentieth century). Japanese immigrants during this time were also ineligible for citizenship and likewise barred from buying property. As a result, their children born on American soil sometimes "owned" their homes in writing, since they could not be denied citizenship.

Throughout this time, the Brotherhood (as the Christian Church was sometimes known in those days) remained consistently committed to Japanese ministry in the United States and to speaking out for the rights of their Japanese brothers and sisters in America. Another *World Call* article spoke about the irony and injustice of a law passed against people who were clearly so "American":

> One day in November, 1923, the United States Supreme Court rendered a decision sustaining the California law which prohibited farming by the Japanese in that state. As the majority of the Japanese in California were engaged in agriculture the decision fell upon them with stunning severity.
>
> The very day when the report of that decision appeared in the papers an American visitor went into

the kindergarten of the Japanese Christian Institute, which is conducted by the United Christian Missionary Society, in Los Angeles, and saw forty-four bright-faced, neatly dressed children of Japanese parents going through their daily exercises. Just at that moment they were concluding the singing of "America." As they completed the national hymn they saluted the flag and repeated in unison and with emphasis: "I pledge allegiance to my flag and to the republic for which it stands, one nation, indivisible, with liberty and justice for all."

It took the visitor a little while to realize the full meaning of that scene. One of its implications appeared two or three years ago when there was talk of war between Japan and the United States. The son of Mr. Kawai ... faced the situation with these words, "Father, if war should come between the United States and Japan, you know I would have to fight on the side of the United States, for I am an American."

Again, one of the leading Christian businessmen of Los Angeles, when told of the kindergarten scene, remarked, "That law will not apply to these children when they grow up. They are just as clearly Americans as our children."

Mr. Kawai's article shows how the Japanese in the United States have met two severe tests. It remains to be seen how well American Christians will meet the one test which arises in their relations with their fellow Christians of Japanese ancestry.[4]

The Japanese Christians of Berkeley faced problems regarding racial hostilities, but the Disciples remained committed to their ecumenical ministry. According to University Christian Church of Berkeley's history:

Through the years the work of the Japanese had been handicapped by an inadequate church home. In 1928 an effort was made to get permission to build a church for the Japanese in Berkeley but the race prejudice was so pronounced in the area that they were refused a permit. The money for the building was available and the plans had been approved and recommended by the city planning commission, but it was refused by the city council because a group of people opposed it. There was no pretense to cover up the fact that the opposition was entirely on the basis of race prejudice. They openly stated that they did not oppose Christian churches—just Japanese![5]

The United Christian Missionary Society (UCMS) leased lots to "Japanese United Church" in 1931 for twenty-five years at an annual rental rate of one dollar "with the privilege of renewal if mutually agreeable," with option to buy later if they so desired. Such a privilege would be impossible to act on within ten years.

Simultaneous to this benchmark for the Japanese United Church in Berkeley, another project for Japanese American Christians was taking root a little to the south. The UCMS noted with pride, "With the completion of a new educational building and church in 1932 the dreams of Mr. Unoura [formerly pastor of the Berkeley church] and all who have ever worked with him in the Japanese Christian Church [of Los Angeles] were realized. According to national authorities ours is the best equipped religious center for Japanese on the Pacific Coast and probably in the United States."[6] A primary focus of the Japanese Christian Institute was to prepare Japanese American children for the American school system and reduce the culture shock that many immigrant children experienced.

At the same time that Disciples were supporting ministry to Japanese immigrants without citizenship rights, their first substantive effort at ministry to the first Americans was gaining steam. The Yakima Mission to Native Americans of the Yakima tribe (a federated tribe of many smaller Native American tribes) focused particularly on a boarding school for children. One of the leaders of this mission wrote the following snapshots of life at the mission:

Teachers in Indian schools say that Indian children in the first and second grades sketch as well as white children in the fifth grade, and that their sense of color and technique of art work are inborn, the natural expression of a racial characteristic to make all things beautiful....

"Herman, lead us in our evening prayer, please?" said Mr. Francis.

There is a moment of absolute silence in preparation, and then a low earnest voice in prayer. Herman understands the needs of his own people and their problems and he prays for better feeling among all the tribes of God's family everywhere. He expresses the gratitude of his heart for the opportunity of knowing Jesus Christ as his friend and counselor and pledges his best efforts to live a Christian life, wherever he may be....

At one corner of the reservation is the Pom Pom Church, in plain sight of the Mission. At another point is the Shaker Indian Church. The Indians who attend these churches are accustomed to direct their worship to the Great Spirit, giver of all power. Their prayers and songs may be to the Sun, to whom they attribute the blessings of harvest and whom they thank for their very existence. The language of the Psalms is familiar to them. Some of their songs are like the Psalms of David. I can think of no holier task for the Disciples of Christ than that of presenting to the American Indian, at this dawning of a better understanding between him and his government, a God who is Father as well as Ruler, and the Christ of the out-of-doors, who understood how to reach the heart of his hearers through stories and patterns, dear to the heart of the Red Man. We are sowing good seed and will some day reap a rich harvest.[7]

The high hopes for Native Americans' strengthened relationship with their government (and, therefore, with God evidently) would not be sustained. The Mission's efforts to reprioritize Yakima values (such as stabilizing family life by not following the fishing patterns but staying in one place all year) were not readily embraced by the Yakima people. But at this early stage, the possibilities of assimilation and Christianization of the Yakima people seemed entirely promising.

In 1920, the Disciples formed, (amidst much controversy over a trend towards centralization, which might mean denominationalism) the United Christian Missionary Society (UCMS). The UCMS provided the resources for ministries such as the Yakima work. While Black Disciples had found the need to form their own support network around the same time, the UCMS saw part of its ministry as functioning to foster relationships with its Black sisters and brothers. Toward this end, the UCMS named Robert H. Peoples "General Secretary of Negro Churches" in 1935. His salary was less than his counterparts. Peoples recalled being told, "Your people don't need as much as we do. You don't have the same expenses."[8]

Japanese were not the only Asian immigrants in the United States, and the Disciples made significant inroads in Los Angeles with the Filipino population during the years preceding World War II, thanks to a fairly progressive ministry philosophy by a White former missionary and the strong leadership of Filipino minister Silvestre Morales. His story is compelling. Morales' eyesight failed him while in seminary in the Philippines: "For years, fearing blindness, he had been memorizing long passages of scripture and scores of hymns."[9]

A White American woman, Mrs. Royal Dye, cooperated with Silvestre Morales and opened her home to the community for social and religious gatherings. She came to be known as "Mother Dye." A former missionary not well enough to travel to the Philippines, Dye chose to invest herself in ministry with the Filipino community in her Los Angeles home instead.

Morales began his work part time, intending to return to the Philippines after getting an education. "After his school hours, he went downtown in the crowded pool halls and other unwholesome places to invite more of his friends and acquaintances to attend the new program sponsored by the Fellowship. In that little garden at the back of Dye's home Filipinos were given a hearty welcome."[10] Morales got himself through seminary in America with the help of his wife reading to him:

> The churches in southern California called him repeatedly and always from their pulpits he sounded a clarion call for deeper consecration and more zealous service. He attended classes in college winning three degrees. Mrs. Morales read to him, otherwise the schoolwork would have been impossible. Special meetings and programs, social affairs, visits in and out, here and there among Filipinos and Americans—days crowded full. But it was Mr. Morales' way. In pool room, boarding house, hotel or in camp among the laborers—everywhere he found the Filipinos who needed help and encouragement.[11]

Part of the success of the Filipino Christian Church was that it offered an outlet (and a source of dignity) for a community that was usually written off by surrounding Whites. It was into this mix of loneliness, isolation, poverty conditions, and lack of spiritual sustenance that the Filipino Christian Church was born. According to Royal Morales : "In 1928, thirteen Filipino students attending the California Christian College, now Chapman University, formed the nucleus of the Filipino Christian Fellowship under the sponsorship of the First Christian Church. In 1933, the Fellowship was formally organized into a church, the Filipino Christian Church."[12]

They soon outgrew this space and moved their Sunday morning activities into First Christian Church.[13] However, afternoon activities occurred at a hall in the heart of Filipino town, offering "band music, drama, native songs, devotional hymns, forum discussions, games, and educational lectures"[14] in contrast to the surrounding pool halls and burlesque shows. The hall was filled to capacity. During the Depression that ensued, non-Filipino giving dropped off, but the Filipino community invested fully in the church.

World War II profoundly affected both Japanese Disciples in America and the White Disciples who had supported their ministries for years. University Christian Church in Berkeley was a perfect example of the tension many Disciples faced between their Christian relationships and American duties. As of 1931, the Japanese Church in Berkeley was no longer officially affiliated with University Christian Church of Berkeley, but they remained in relationship. Idalene Raab's church history notes, "They shared, too, in the heartache as University Christian Church opened its doors to them for the last time—as an Evacuation Center when war hysteria made it necessary for all Japanese of the Pacific Coast to be evacuated in 1941."[15]

Before the evacuation of Japanese Americans to concentration camps scattered throughout the United States, it had already become clear to Japanese American Disciples that things were changing. K. Kubota, a leader in the Japanese Christian Institute in Los Angeles, wrote on March 14, 1941: "As you know, the world condition is getting worse, and the relation between Japan and America is developing in an ungodly way. Only mutual understanding and harmony in Christ lead us toward the true light. It is the time to bear our own crosses for the sake of humanity."[16] Shortly after this, a number of men in the church were taken into custody to be examined, leaving the wives to carry on business. Many had lost jobs or customers. Likewise, the assets of Japanese institutions (including the Japanese Christian Institute) were frozen. The church tried to stay afloat amidst these pressures. In a letter in December of that year, the leaders wrote:

Although business assets and credits have loosened up, the bank account of organizations have not been lifted. It means that we cannot touch our Institute account at the present time. We are keeping up our Kindergarten; our Language School is suspended; the church work is going on about the same except club activities are suspended since we cannot have night meetings.[17]

Two years after this struggle, toward the end of the internment process, the minister of Japanese Christian Institute summed up the experience in *World Call*:

Life is filled with surprises and reverses, and it is not always rosy or inviting. May 9, 1942, was the most fateful day for the life of the Japanese Christian Church and Institute of Los Angeles, for on that day nearly forty years of concerted effort of Disciples of Christ abruptly came to an end. What a tragic day it was for all of us who love the Lord! When we think about it, it makes us sick at heart. Yet, it is said that every cloud has a silver lining. For those of us who believe in God as the source of our ultimate destiny, it was the beginning of a greater chapter in Christian experience. [18]

White Disciples were aware of the challenges their Japanese American brothers and sisters faced during the process leading up to internment. In the influential periodical *World Call*, a cover editorial appeared in 1942 bemoaning the plight of Japanese Disciples.

Various Christian bodies of America—among them the Disciples of Christ—have seen one of the great opportunities in the field of home missions in work among large racial groups not wholly assimilated into our common life and culture ... It has brought blessing both to those whom it served and to those from whose hearts it sprang.

An example of this type of home missions is the work of the United Christian Missionary Society among the Japanese in the Japanese Christian Institute and the Japanese Christian Church in Los Angeles, California. Christian people who have loved that work through the years have in recent weeks experienced many heartaches as they have learned of the sorrow and suffering which have come to thousands of innocent people of Japanese origin–among them some who through all their lives have lived under the goodly influence of these Christian institutions on the West Coast.

That this situation could not be wholly otherwise does not lessen the sense of regret which we feel; nor does it relieve us of our own continuing responsibility for carrying through on a great task to which we are committed. [19]

The editorial continues: "It is good to know of the valiant way in which our ministers and others in California are seeing to it that Christian friendship is not wanting in this hour of distress.[20] It is likewise gratifying to learn of the efforts of government representatives (including agents of the Federal Bureau of Investigation) to be fair, though altogether thorough in their efforts to deal with a problem which all must admit is complex."[21]

Not all Disciples found the evacuation process "fair yet thorough." Maureen Osuga was a child at the mostly-White Alhambra Christian Church when her family left for the internment camps. Osuga shares the following story:

> I was born to a pharmacist father and a Phi Beta Kappa mother who was denied a teaching position although jobs were available…Our family was upwardly mobile until December 7, 1941. Then I was compelled to leave my dolls, stuffed animals, frilly dresses, toy refrigerator and stove, swing, outdoor playhouse and

all my playmates to dwell in a one-room tar-papered hovel.[22]

The family was initially incarcerated at the Santa Anita race track, where some stayed in unclean horse stables. The members of her church embraced Osuga and supported her throughout the process, but the problem did not seem complex nor the process fair yet thorough.

Disciples reached out to one another during this time, but a system of discrimination still punished Japanese Disciples for crimes uncommitted. Despite harsh conditions, however, Japanese Disciples ministry did not stop in the internment camps. Kojiro Unoura wrote in great detail about years of intentional work he did in cooperation with the UCMS, including one particular effort while interned in Colorado:

> In cooperation with the Colorado Christian Missionary Society, the United Christian Missionary Society appointed me, beginning July 1, 1943, to serve, in the capacity of pastor at large, the people of Japanese ancestry who live in the Arkansas Valley of Southern Colorado. I was definitely instructed by both societies not to start any segregated racial church, but to work on the principal of integration, encouraging our people to attend the existing Caucasian churches. This has been done with the hearty cooperation of all Christian ministers in the valley … We have a very fine relationship with the local Christian church. Its minister, C. E. Root, extends the right hand of fellowship on behalf of the church to all people of Japanese ancestry. Our young people freely mix with the Caucasian young people both in Christian Endeavor meetings and on social occasions. Just this summer five young people from our group attended the summer conferences. During the year just closed, four people were baptized and joined the local church.[23]

This story highlights the challenge and the gift of multicultural ministry at this time: multicultural ministry meant non-Whites assimilating into White churches. It also meant relationships between Whites and Japanese Americans sometimes broke down the ugly and abusive stereotypes about Japanese Americans dominant in America at the time.

While the Disciples' 1944 resolution asked for an end to the internment process, it made no mention of the role of racism. Rather it focused on the notion that internment had served its purpose and was no longer necessary. Not all Disciples took the same position. While Disciples generally agreed on the necessity of charity toward those in internment camps, some Disciples (including the members of the Alhambra Church that Maureen Osuga attended) believed an element of justice was also necessary. Joseph B. Hunter served as Assistant Director at Rohwer Relocation Center from 1942–1944. By 1946, he was the National Director for Peace and Interracial Understanding in the department of social welfare for the United Christian Missionary Society. He wrote a strongly-worded racial analysis of the failures of the relocation program in *World Call*. Hunter listed eight observations about the process that highlighted his thoughts about internment policies in general, as well as the role of Disciples. Here are several of his reflections at that time:

> 4. The evacuation presented the country with a new group of saboteurs–the people who wanted to get rid of the Japanese Americans as competitors. Their hysterical demand for evacuation was the culmination of years of race-baiting. They helped to deprive the country of food producers, war workers and good soldiers ...

> 6. The evacuation reveals the fragile nature of our constitutional guarantees of "liberty and justice for all." ...

> 7. The evacuation experience is not all loss. Providence will use it for the nation's good. It has made American

Christians more conscious of the sin of racism than they have ever been before. Race prejudice is an insult to God who made us of one blood. We can have race discrimination or democracy but we cannot have both.

Another gain from the evacuation is the educational benefit which it brought to hosts of Americans who live in parts of our country where an Oriental has seldom appeared. The resettlement of Americans of Japanese descent in every state is helping to prepare thousands of Americans to live in the world of today and tomorrow …

8. A final observation is that a free church, even in wartime, can come to the aid of a minority group caught in a situation which results in discrimination and injustice. In this case, even though others helped, it was the church which provided help and sympathy from the first. Christian churches within the relocation centers were the one strong morale agency that helped to hold the people together. Christians among the evacuees found outside jobs and worked for community acceptance. It was the church and church-supported publications that presented to the nation and to Congress the true story of this unfortunate episode in American life.[24]

Unfortunately, the end of the internment camps was not the end of struggles for Japanese American Disciples.

After the War

In the words of Disciples historian Timothy Lee, eventually the Japanese Christian Institute in Los Angeles could not hold its tenuous grip on its church. During World War II, along with 120,000 other Japanese-Americans living on the West Coast, members of Japanese Christian Church- were herded into internment camps. Their church was no more. Church property was taken over by the denomination and became the basis for All Peoples Church (Disciples of Christ). With the war over, returning members of defunct Japanese Christian Church were invited to join All Peoples Church. Some did, but many wished to reconstitute themselves into a distinctly Japanese-American church.[25]

In West Adams' own telling of their history:

> Our West Adams Christian Church is 54 years old. However, our mother church, the Japanese Christian Church began in 1908, 97 years ago ... The Social Hall in the basement, the Chapel on the first floor; and the upper floors were apartments where members lived.... When WWII ended and the Japanese Americans returned, our church was not returned. The four Japanese Christian Churches were discontinued and we were advised to join Caucasian churches. However, many of the Japanese did not understand English. Finally, the Disciples allowed one church to be established in 1948, this church.[26]

Built in 1950, the West Adams Christian Church moved into the Crenshaw area of Los Angeles to connect with the many Japanese families there. The church at first grew significantly, then as the neighborhood changed and fewer second and third generation Japanese stayed in the area, membership began to dwindle. Japanese language services were discontinued in 2004, as the few remaining first generation Japanese members of the congregation aged and died. As of this book's publication, there are 40 members now, many between the ages of 70 and 90.

Kay Kokubun (son of Jingoro Kokubun) was one of the Japanese members who returned to the newly-formed All Peoples Christian Church. Of Japanese-American parentage, Kokubun was sent from his home in California to a relocation center at Poston, Arizona, at the beginning of World War II. In 1944 he was helped in separating from the center by funds from the Emergency Million raised in the Christian Churches. With the help of these funds, he entered Drake University in Des Moines, Iowa. After the war, Kokubun completed his undergraduate study at Chapman College in Los Angeles. In 1951 he received a bachelor degree in divinity from the Pacific School of Religion in Berkeley, California.[27] While in Des Moines, he was told the Disciples would support his education, but he wouldn't get a job in a Disciples church because there was only one Japanese Christian church, and the denomination's goal was integrated, multicultural churches (which, it went without saying, could not possibly be pastored by a Japanese American minister). Despite this warning, Kokubun joined the staff of All Peoples in June, 1951 as minister to young people in the church and community center. He was ordained in October 1951 and installed as pastor in September 1956.[28] When Kay felt he was reaching the end of his effectiveness at All Peoples, he decided to seek another pastorate in the Disciples but was told (as was David Unora, the son of the West Adams pastor) that there was no place for him to serve since there were no available Japanese churches. This was said with full knowledge that Pastor Kokobun's leadership experience had been in a multicultural context. Eventually both Pastor Unora and Pastor Kokubun left the denomination.[29]

In the rebuilding era of early post-war America, not a great deal of ministry to and with non-White Disciples shows up on the radar beyond the stories of Japanese Americans quietly integrating themselves into White churches in their new home cities. (many Japanese Americans had been relocated away from the coasts during this time). In fact, according to Daisy Machado, "between 1945–1995 thirteen Hispanic churches were started in Texas, two of which are no longer in existence. Of these thirteen almost all were initiated by Latino Disciples, none of whom were born in the United States."[30] Disciples continued to wrestle with how to do ministry to and with American Latinos in their own local context. One notable change in this area, however, was that E.G. Luna, Mexican-born Disciples minister educated at

Texas Christian University, came to head the previously White-led Inman Center in 1944.[31] At the same time, Puerto Rican ministries in mainland United States were about to blossom with the birth of its flagship church.

La Hermosa Christian Church was the first Hispanic Disciples congregation established in New York. La Hermosa was established in 1939 by an independent group of Puerto Rican immigrants. At the very beginning, the congregation was not related to the Disciples. However, through contacts with the Disciples in Puerto Rico, the congregation became a Disciples congregation in 1943 after securing the services of Pablo Cotto, who came originally from Dajaos Christian Church, the second oldest Disciples congregation in Puerto Rico.[32] As a pamphlet from the church in the 1950s tells the story,

> Late in the 1930's, Puerto Rican families came to New York in increasing numbers in search of jobs. A young seminary student was among them. He saw fellow Puerto Ricans settling in the slums of New York and realized that they needed the Christian ministry there more than they ever needed it before.
>
> The student minister called together several families who had been evangelical Christians back home on the island. They held prayer meetings in a tenement room. Then, in 1938, a handful of people organized La Hermosa church. La Hermosa means "beautiful." It was a good name for a church in the dirty slum, because Christian fellowship and the word of God can bring something beautiful into the lives of people.
>
> The congregation grew and began to overtax the tenement apartment. Neighbors complained of "so many people going up and down the stairs." After a few years, the little band of Christians needed a building of their own. They also wanted to tie themselves to a larger church body. Some had been Disciples of Christ on the island. In 1944, La Hermosa asked to become a

part of the Disciples of Christ and was accepted into the brotherhood. The church located a four-story building on East 110th Street in Harlem and undertook to buy it. The structure was only twenty feet wide and was hemmed in by crumbling old tenements. But it would be a church home.[33]

At the same time Puerto Rican Disciples were beginning their journey with White Disciples in the United States, Black Disciples faced a crossroads about remaining affiliated with White Disciples:

Meeting in Lexington, Kentucky, in 1944, the National Christian Missionary Convention [the body of the Black Disciples] voted to expand their partnership with the United Christian Missionary Society [a major arm of the predominantly White Disciples]. That action drew many black Disciples into the Movement's heated discussion over the practice of "open membership."[34] Sere Stacy Myers (1898-2000), the presiding president of the NCMC, and Robert Hayes Peoples, a former National field program director, made extensive field trips to sponsor orientation forums among the by then more than 500 predominantly black congregations related to the NCMC. Most congregations maintained affiliation with the NCMC.[35]

Established to give Black Disciples autonomy in the wake of the Civil War, the Assembly churches of the eastern seaboard continued to worship within their own structures. White Disciples began to lose contact with Assembly churches as early as 1901. According to one former bishop of the Assembly churches from the 1970s, "White Disciples organized black Disciples and assisted us in every way until we got our first black leader, and then turned us loose. They withdrew from us and there was no communication between us and them for many decades. But when they came back, they found something," noted former bishop James L. Melvin. In an article for *The Disciple*, Melvin notes,

> What white Disciples found was that the black Disciples had associated with Free Will Baptists and other denominations since their departure and had adopted some of their practices. Notable were the washing of feet as a continuation of the Lord's Supper (enacted every three months), bimonthly worship services, bi-vocational ministers, a literalistic view of Scripture, longer and sometimes more lively worship services, an organizational structure that includes bishops, and churches named after saints and places in the Bible.[36]

Talks began in the early 1940s between the groups, with White pastors going to Black ministers' homes, since they could not meet in public places in North Carolina in the 1940s and it was safer for Whites to go to Black neighborhoods than the other way around. The conversations were fairly smooth in these early days, although they would break down in the 1950s and 1960s, with wounds it would take decades to heal.

As work of integration, assimilation, compromise, and new life occurred among Disciples of color during this period, the Yakima Indian Christian Mission work continued to move at a slow or perhaps even pace. White mission workers expressed their frustration about the pace of life among the indigenous people in the following way in 1949, still through the lens of the white man's burden:

> We cannot hurry the Indian. Three hundred years seems a long time for us to get acquainted with him. Surely, from 1620 down to date is time enough for us to have Christianized him, assimilated him, wooed him, and won him. But, there were few who cared about him, and fewer still who worked with him. At first we fought him as an enemy; later we looked on him as a nuisance. He, then, as Merriam says, became our problem. Only later did we take him as our responsibility.

Out here in the Northwest we have known the Yakima Indian for less than a hundred years. We Disciples of Christ began to work with his children twenty or thirty years ago. We have only scratched the surface, but we have made a beginning. But, the Indian is slow. And we can move him only as fast as he wants to go ....

Our service is simple and informal. Sometimes we use the Balopticon to illustrate the lesson. The Indian is confused with a complicated gospel. We have started! Pray for us as we visit the homes, and invite them to our services.[37]

The even pace and negotiations of living together in the wake of World War II would set the scene for an intentionally integrative approach to ministry by Disciples in the third quarter of the century.

Notes

[1]Ben E. Watson, "A 'Yellow Peril' or 'Golden Opportunity'?" *World Call* (August 1926): 29. Watson spent a term as a missionary in Japan; at the time of this article's publication, he served as superintendent of work among "Orientals" on the Pacific Coast.

[2]Idalene M. Raab, *The Christian Church (Disciples of Christ) at work in Berkeley, 1893–1968* (published by the author, 1968), 110.

[3]Suzunosuke Kato, "Interracial Fellowship in Berkeley," *World Call* (November 1924): 38.

[4]"Americans All," *World Call* (January 1924): 52.

[5]Raab, *at Work in Berkeley,* 118–19.

[6]Information taken from a brief biography by the United Christian Missionary Society in 1934.

[7]Lucy King DeMoss, "You Really Should Visit the Yakima Mission," *World Call* (September 1928): 6–7.

[8]Joseph S. Saunders, "Black Disciples Are Moving: Out of the Balcony, Into the Main Auditorium," undated monograph, 16.

[9]"Silvestre Morales," in *Biography set: Sketches of certain ones of our missionaries, our missionary leaders, workers in the national churches,* series 1, leaflet 14 (Indianapolis, Department of Missionary Education, UCMS, 1933).

[10]Severino F. Corpus, "An Analysis of the Racial Adjustment Activities and Problems of the Filipino-American Christian Fellowship in Los Angeles" (dissertation, University of Southern California, 1938), 36.

[11]Biography of Morales by United Christian Missionary Society, 1933.

[12]Royal F. Morales, *Makibaka 2: The Philipino American Struggle* (Los Angeles: Mountainview Publishers, 1974), 216.

64 Room at the Table

[13]In 1950 the church relocated to its own property in a permanent location in Filipino Town.

[14]Corpus, "Analysis," 37.

[15]Raab, *at Work in Berkeley,* 121.

[16]A quotation from the Japanese Christian Church files at the Disciples Historical Society.

[17]K. Unoura and K. Kuboto, letter in response to inquiry from Rev. W. F. Learned, December 16, 1941.

[18]Kojiro Unura, "Christian Ministry in Exile," *World Call* (November 1944): 19–21.

[19]Cover editorial, *World Call* (April 1942): 1.

[20]Interviews with Maureen Osuga and Aki Suzuki, the history of University Christian Church in Berkeley, and letters from Kojiro Unoura during his internment bear out that White Disciples did reach out to Japanese American Disciples in the camps wherever there had been preexisting relationships.

[21]*World Call* editorial.

[22]Maureen Shashihara Osuga, undated essay for newsletter for Bazetta Christian Church, Cortland, Ohio.

[23]Unoura, "Christian Ministry in Exile," 19–21. This understanding of integration as a process of incorporating non-Whites into Anglo churches would have significant impact on Unoura's ministry when the camps closed, as well as on the ministries of his son and of Disciples pastor Kay Kokubun, discussed in the next chapter. It is hard to estimate how many ministries were shaped or misshaped by the denomination's unofficial policy of assimilation as the road to multicultural ministry.

[24]Joseph B. Hunter, "Would We Do It Again? Looking Now at the Japanese American Evacuation," *World Call* (March 1946): 22–23.

[25]Timothy S. Lee, "West Adams Christian Church (Disciples of Christ)," *NAPAD Newsletter* 22, no. 2 (Winter 1999–2000): 5.

[26]Joe Nagano, "West Adams Christian Church, May 2005," unpublished white paper.

[27]UCMS biography, May 1963.

[28]Personal interview on February 9, 2006. Upon his departure from All Peoples Christian Church, Rev. Kokubun was unable to secure another ministry position anywhere within in the denomination. He became a leader in Asian American activism on the West Coast and worships at a multicultural United Church of Christ.

[29]In 2004, Pacific Southwest Regional Minister Don Shelton awarded Kay Kokobun the region's annual MLK award and also offered a formal apology to Kokobun on behalf of the region.

[30]Daisy Machado, "From Ango-American [sic] Traditions to a Multicultural World," *Discipliana* 57 (Summer 1997), 54.

[31]Taken from a UCMS biography of E.G. Luna written in February 1964.

[32]Pablo A. Jiménez, "Hispanics in the Movement," in *The Encyclopedia of the Stone-Campbell Movement,* ed. Douglas A. Foster, Paul M. Blowers, Anthony L Dunnavant, and D. Newell Williams (Grand Rapids, Mich.: William B. Eerdmans, 2004), 396.

[33]"A Church That Grew...With The Odds Against It," flyer published probably by UCMS after 1956, around the time that the church was about to be displaced because of slum clearance.

[34]Open membership was the idea that you did not need to be bodily immersed in order for you to transfer membership to a Disciples of Christ Church. The issue was largely resolved by the 1960s, although Disciples congregational polity means that the very occasional Disciples church might still invite or encourage re-baptism even today.

[35]William K. Fox Sr., "African Americans in the Movement," in *Encyclopedia*, 13.

[36]Londia R. Darden, "Disciples, Too!" *The Disciple* (December 1985): 18.

[37]M. L. Norment, White Swan, Washington, "A Slow, Patient People–the Indian," *World Call* (October 1949): 47. This was a letter to the editor.

5

Unity in Diversity?
1950–1975

The 1960s retain a certain infamy for radical action and civil rights, spawning feminism, Black Power, the Chicano movement, and even Asian identity movements in the United States. What remains fascinating about Disciples history is that during the late 1960s, a time when even the greatest advocates of integration were beginning to despair of America's capacity to overcome its divides—when integrationist movements were being replaced by separatist movements (e.g. the transition of the Student Non-violent Coordinating Committee under the leadership of Stokely Carmichael)—Black Disciples intentionally chose a path of merger, of uniting the body of Christ. Simultaneously, while Latino Disciples demanded their voices be heard, they also remained part of the predominantly White Disciples movement.

Perhaps a combination of post-war concerns among Asian Americans and lack of immigration options resulted in their lack of activity among Disciples during this era. West Adams Christian Church was established in the wake of Japanese internment after serious negotiations with UCMS, according to Geunhee Yu, but "for the next three decades, the Disciples' Asian ministry remained fairly dormant until a great wave of new immigrants from Asia came under the new Immigration Acts of 1965."[1] Another possibility is that the emphasis on "multicultural ministry" focused on White leadership, limiting opportunities for ministry by Asian Americans in a racially-segregated United States.[2]

During this era little changed regarding Disciples' inter-actions with Native Americans as well. As one Disciple wrote in a mid-1950s issue of *World Call:*

> It is embarrassing for us to review the effort we have made on behalf of the Indians. Disciples have one home for Indian children and one church. When we add a small annual financial gift to the Indian program of the Division of Home Missions of the National Council of Churches, we have the picture of our program for the Indians—100,000 of them.[3]

At the same time that little was happening on the home front regarding Asian ministries, the seeds planted abroad with Disciples mission work began to bring forth fruit that would have an impact in the United States. Two concrete examples are that on September 28, 1956, the UCMS commissioned Itoko Maeda, a Japanese native and graduate of College of the Bible (now Lexington Theological Seminary), to open a new mission field in Okinawa and serve as a missionary there.[4] While serving there, she reported stories back to the United States, including a description of a farewell party for a fellow missionary:

> Many church members gathered to say farewell and expressed appreciation for his work. They felt that his years on the island had been a great help. A note of realism was added by a man of 70 years from a country church: "Since many Americans live on Okinawa, we have seen many Americans. Some of them are very

fine people, but some are terribly bad. You tell us you are going back to America as a missionary. Many Americans don't know God and Christ is our Lord. Please tell them about God and Christ so they may find real Christian living."[5]

Itoko Maeda served as a missionary from the United States back to her homeland of Japan (she would continue to do mission work to Japanese people displaced to South America, and then work with White Americans in the United States throughout her career).

One of the key leaders of Asian American Disciples was in formation at this time—Soongook Choi. Converted to Christianity in his homeland of Korea in 1946, he learned of Disciples there and was baptized in 1953. He started a church for refugees in Seoul in 1953 and then attended Vanderbilt Divinity School.[6] His decision to stay in the United States rather than going home to establish new churches in Korea would later change the face of Disciplesdom. Simultaneously, another future leader of Asian Disciples, David Kagiwada, began seminary at the University of Chicago Divinity School. After leaving the Poston, Arizona, internment camps, he initially embarked on training in social work; but he was told the questions he was asking were being answered in divinity school. His ministry and Soongook Choi's together would create a voice for Asian Disciples within the larger Disciples community. But in the 1950s and 60s, that voice remained fairly faint.

White Disciples were aware of the relevance of the Latino community in the United States in the 1950s, a community where the Disciples had made few strides. However, the efforts of Latino Disciples themselves to begin Spanish language ministries placed the issue on a front burner for many, including the Disciples Division of Homeland Ministries. One *World Call* article in 1953 noted:

Pastors and lay leaders of several Spanish-speaking churches are reaching out with missionary ventures of their own...It is not practical for the Spanish speaking churches to consider establishing many mission outposts, for another critical problem stands in their way. There is an almost complete lack of young ministers coming on to serve new churches. The monthly stipend now received by most of the Spanish-speaking pastors does not entice young men who have graduated from high school and can earn more in trades and industries....

Minority peoples make heavy demands upon their spiritual leaders. The Mexican and Puerto Rican congregations in the United States need the skilled guidance of pastors trained in counseling and social service as well as in evangelism. Spanish-speaking pastors must know how to call upon the services of community agencies. They must be able to work with Anglo-Americans in the community in order to serve effectively as mission pastors. For such work they need training beyond that given in undergraduate Bible institutes.[7]

One church that had begun to respond to social as well as spiritual needs was La Hermosa, by this time flourishing in Harlem. According to literature from the congregation at the time:

A big city slum is an ugly place. The Puerto Rican settlement in Harlem is known as one of New York City's worst sections. Apartments built to house five families are cut into rooms for twenty families. A single bathroom with ancient plumbing and no hot water serves thirty or more persons.

Children grow up in Harlem with no place to play but the busy streets. Working adults often suffer discrimination at the hands of employers, unions and landlords.

In this setting La Hermosa Christian Church flourished. The Puerto Ricans are zealous evangelists

and generous in their giving. They do not forget the
habits of church membership which they learned from
missionaries.[8]

Their stewardship results from sixty years of Disciples
of Christ mission work in Puerto Rico. They have
accomplished what other Protestant groups have not
done recently in New York—evangelize successfully and
plant new churches.[9]

With these types of ministries and with increasing numbers
of Latino ministers starting Disciples churches, the Rev. Byron
Spice began to seek ways to respond to the needs and demands
of Latino ministries as the director of Homeland Missions
for the UCMS. Spice did this with a goal of assimilation and
acculturation. Daisy Machado states that in the 1928 Disciples
Survey of Service included the following comment:

Why should we seek to bring Christ to the Spanish-
speaking people in the United States? We are not only
under obligation to our Lord to make Christians of
these people, but we also have a patriotic obligation to
make of them good citizens for our fair nation.

Machado goes on to note:

While this is not a very surprising statement for the
1920s, what is surprising is that thirty-eight years later,
in 1964, Spice continues to echo the same mentality.
He writes:

Growth in acculturation… is certainly one of the
desired outcomes of our ministry to Spanish-speaking
people… The Spanish-language churches provide a
training ground where Spanish-speaking person can
prepare themselves to take their places as members
and possible leaders in English-speaking churches…
Perhaps the goal of our work is to bring about such a
degree of acculturation that eventually all will worship
in English-speaking churches.

What one notices immediately is that the ultimate denominational goal was not the creation of strong, self-sufficient, self-governing Latino congregations. Instead the emphasis is on the creation of 'bridge' congregations that would help Latino immigrants 'cross over' to the dominant culture. These "bridge congregations" would then die after completing their task. [10]

Spice laid out a notion of "mission churches" in 1966 whereby congregations could be set up to minister to (and presumably be led by) ethnic expressions of the church in partnership with state, district, and national expressions: "A Mission Church will continue as long as its mission is needed. However, each church shall seek constant growth in Christian witness, program and stewardship."[11]

In that same year, Spice called together Hispanic ministers for the first time. During that consultation, the following recommendation was given:

So long as education, acculturation and integration are part of the American way of life, mission churches will search out, evangelize, educate, acculturate and graduate its members, but they will not become a separate "sister church." With the constant loss of leadership and financial strength they cannot be expected to become financially independent.

The Church of Jesus Christ in the United States is ONE. This is the ideal and we work toward it. We do not work toward the establishment of a separate National Spanish Church.[12]

"Although he repeated there his mistaken idea that Hispanic congregations were to be bridges that would solely facilitate the integration of Spanish-speaking people to Anglo-European congregations," writes Pablo Jiménez, "the meeting gave Hispanic leaders and opportunity to network in ways never done before."[13] This opportunity fostered a powerful movement that would eventually become the Hispanic Bilingual Fellowship and the Central Pastoral Office on Hispanic Ministries.

Other "firsts" occurred in 1966. John Compton, a prominent Black Disciples minister was appointed assistant regional minister in Ohio, that state's first ethnic minority regional staff person. Just as there were costs to trying to retain an ethnic identity in a mostly-White church, there were costs to striving to serve in an integrated church, including Compton's Cleveland house burning while he attended a state convention. Compton's experience did not slow his commitment either to fighting for racial justice or to serving the mostly-White denomination in a long series of "firsts." John Compton was the first African American to serve as regional minister (Indiana 1979–81), as well as the first African American to serve as president of a division (Homeland Ministries from 1982–89).[14]

Probably the most significant moment in the integration of the church was dawning at this point. In 1969, the National Convention formally merged with the predominantly-Anglo Disciples body. The process, born of a commitment to integration, began in 1959 with the discontinuation of National Convention program responsibilities. It concluded with the dissolution of the National Convention and the International Convention (a mostly-White body) into the General Assembly.[15]

At the 53rd National Christian Missionary Convention annual assembly in August 1969, NCMC President Raymond Brown explained what was at stake:

> We meet representing what may be called a predom-
> inantly Black Convention seeking to implement a
> merger with what may be called a predominantly White
> Convention. We meet at a time when it is unpopular
> for Black people to be anything short of proponents of
> separateness; when it is popular to create unrest; when
> tensions between peoples are mounting higher and
> higher; when there are those who want to be where
> the action is, and yet be true, faithful and just to the

principles and heritage of those who established both the Church and the National Christian Missionary Convention; but more especially Him to whom we have committed our lives.[16]

This letter was followed by greetings from the Convention's first president, Edith Richardson, who wrote "At a time when repatriation and Black Power are the watchwords, we are meeting to talk about making real the unity of God's Church. We come to this meeting aware that God knows and agrees that 'Black is Beautiful.' Yet, we who are Christians cannot forget that the church has the responsibility of bringing all men to full brotherhood under God."[17]

At the exact moment when many African Americans were giving up on White America's capacity to live into the Beloved Community of Martin Luther King's dream, Black Disciples chose to merge with White Disciples because they were so committed to Disciples' core value of unity in the body of Christ that they were willing to take the risks involved,(and they would have plenty of disappointments over time, but they would remain a part of the larger whole.

The year1969 was also the year that "Byron Spice called Domingo Rodríguez to serve as director of the Office of Programs and Services for Hispanic and Bilingual Congregations of the Division of Homeland Ministries of the United Missionary Society. Rodríguez was the first Hispanic to serve in such a capacity."[18] In a very short period of time, Disciples managed a significant shift toward both unity with and increased dignity of communities on the margins.

In 1967, reconciliation was introduced to the wider church. In 1968, the Disciples established the Urban Emergency Program in response to the burning of many major metropolitan communities. In 1969, however, a document called "The Black Manifesto" changed the dialogue about religion and race in America. The document demanded that churches offer $500 million in reparations for their complicity in the oppression of Black Americans. The Black Manifesto shook up several denominations regarding their positions on race relations, and the Christian Church (Disciples of Christ) responded strongly. At the 1969 General Assembly in Seattle (the same one that finalized the merger between the International Convention and the National Christian Missionary Convention), the Disciples passed a resolution about its failures in this area:

> We confess that though we call ourselves Christians, we have been timid about the ugly sin of white racism which has now begotten the corresponding sin of black racism.
>
> We acknowledge that despite our resolutions and pronouncements, our churches have, with rare exception, failed to demonstrate a raceless Christianity, a community of once alienated persons reconciled and made one in Christ.
>
> We repent our racism, we pledge ourselves by God's grace to bring forth the fruits of repentance.[19]

The church called for all of its agencies to deploy ten percent of their operating and capital funds for programs dealing with "urban crisis and minority needs" for four years, and to set a goal of having minorities comprise 20 percent of staff by 1975.

By 1972 it became clear that racism was not going to disappear in the next few years. Reconciliation became "a long range commitment of the church," with racial reconciliation still at the heart of the Disciples' stated goals for the church today.

Just after the Disciples wrestled with the impact of the Black Manifesto on their ministries, Hispanic Disciples ministers gathered in 1970–thirty-eight ministers from eleven states, as well as Puerto Rico and Mexico. They created a list of recommendations that included a permanent conference of Hispanic ministers with financial assistance from the general church, scholarships for Hispanic ministerial candidates, Spanish-language resources to be published in Christian education, and that Hispanics elect their own representatives to the denomination's Board and Administrative Committee.[20]

By 1973 this gathering would be open to laypeople as well, and by 1979 it was known as the "Hispanic Encounter."[21]

The development of identity within the Asian American community would take a considerably different form:

> In 1972, Harold Johnson, of the Disciples' Division of Homeland Ministries, visited Thailand and, amid the water buffalo gently nibbling the lush rice stalks and the sounds of chimes singing in the breeze, developed an affinity with the Thais, and his "Asian soul" was born. Upon Johnson's return to Indiana, he urged Homeland Ministries to host an informal consultation with Asian Disciples.[22]

Over the years, Johnson would continue to play a crucial role in advocating for and with Asian Disciples. When Asian American Disciples today talk about their biennial gatherings, they sometimes mention Harold Johnson's role in the movement as part of the reason their gatherings include many people of other races—because their founding was assisted so extensively by a White leader in the church.

At the time only a blip on the radar, the beginnings of Disciples' relationships with Haitian Christians in the United States also began at this time:

> Evangelical Crusade Fishers of Men Christian Church was started in 1973 by Philius Nicolas, himself a Haitian who became a Disciple in 1976 and a U.S. citizen in 1978. "I had thought I was going to start an independent church," says Mr. Nicolas. "I was attending Union Theological Seminary here in New York when I read a book that had all of the different denominational histories in it. I liked what I read about Alexander Campbell's theology and so I began writing letters. Bill Nottingham from the Division of Overseas Ministries put me in touch with Art Stanley, who was the regional minister at the time. Art brought me in. He taught me the Disciples way of doing things. In 1974 the ball

started rolling and by 1976 I was a Disciple and I tell you that I always will be," says Mr. Nicolas.[23]

By the turn of the millennium, this would be one of the fastest growing minority communities within the Disciples.

Key Disciples leader Lucas Torres wrote an extensive paper on the role of Latinos within the Disciples Movement in 1974. Reflecting on a statement by Byron Spice from the 1966 consultation, in which Spice called for Hispanic churches to serve as a bridge for assimilation into White culture and language, Torres observed:

> The Disciples of Christ grew in the historical context of the expansion to the West. The newborn religious movement soon caught the spirit of the frontier: the sense of adventure and exploration, the will to build and open new ways, the risk in the face of the future, the flexibility and spontaneity in all areas of endeavor. Today the Disciples, as many other denominations, are facing a new frontier in its own organizational sphere. But a wider and rapidly expanding frontier is challenging the church of today: the new socio-cultural scene in which a great amalgam of sub-cultures and ethnic groups collide and interact exploring the way of the future. The Church should be able to look with faith at the historical hour and with the boldness of the beginning fulfill its ministry of reconciliation.[24]

Perhaps the work of these crucial years began to pave the path for the fulfillment of that vision.

Notes

[1]Geunhee Yu, "Asian American Disciples," in *The Encyclopedia of the Stone-Campbell Movement,* ed. Douglas A. Foster, Paul M. Blowers, Anthony L Dunnavant, and D. Newell Williams (Grand Rapids, Mich.: William B. Eerdmans, 2004), 40.

[2]Japanese Disciples returning from internment were told to merge into White Disciples churches. It is possible the denomination strategically chose, in the wake of internment, not to invest in specifically Asian ministries.

[3]Fred W. Michel, "Disciples and America's Minorities," *World Call* (July-August 1956): 15.

[4]"Three Young People Commissioned for Overseas Missionary Service," (November 1956), from Itoko Maeda's biographical file, Disciples Historical Society, Nashville.

[5]"Progress, Problems in Okinawa," a newspaper article of September 1958 from Itoko Maeda's biographical file at the Disciples Historical Society. The original publisher of the article is unknown.

[6]Soongook Choi, biographical sketch, *Tennessee Christian,* undated, 4.

[7]Louise Moseley, "A Fertile Field for the Church," *World Call* (June 1953): 19–20.

[8]Interestingly, at this same time a story was reported about the contrast between the Puerto Rican Second Christian Church, nesting with an Anglo congregation. The Anglo congregation expressed frustration that it could only raise one-tenth of what the Latino church raised, even though it was one-half the size of the Latino church.

[9]"A Church That Grew…With The Odds Against It," flyer published probably by UCMS after 1956, around the time that the church was about to be displaced because of slum clearance.

[10]Daisy Machado, "From Ango-American [sic] Traditions to a Multicultural World," *Discipliana* 57 (Summer 1997), 55–56.

[11]Byron L. Spice, "Summary Report of the Spanish Work Consultation," (July 13, 1966), 6.

[12]Lucas Torres, *Struggle for Dignity: Hispanic Americans and their relationship to the Churches in the United States,* (1974), 83, quoting the report on "The Spanish Work Consultation," (Indianapolis: Department of Home Mission Ministries, United Christian Missionary Society, 1966) 65.

[13]Pablo A. Jiménez, "Hispanics in the Movement," in *Encyclopedia,* 397.

[14]Robert L. Friedly, "The way paver," *The Disciple* (June 1991): 4.

[15]William K. Fox, "Before You Begin," in *The Untold Story: A Short History of Black Disciples* (St. Louis: Christian Board of Publication, 1976), 4.

[16]From address by Brown at National Christian Missionary Convention 53rd Assembly, August 5-10, 1969, Transylvania University, Lexington, Kentucky.

[17]Ibid.

[18]Jiménez, "Hispanics," 397.

[19]Joseph S. Saunders, "Black Disciples Are Moving: Out of the Balcony, Into the Main Auditorium," undated monograph, 16.

[20]David Vargas, "A Historical Background of the National Hispanic and Bilingual Fellowship," *Discipliana* 46 (Fall 1986): 40.

[21]Ibid.

[22]Janet Casey-Allen, "Disciples of Asian origin vie for their place," *The Disciple* (May 1994): 9.

[23]Londia R. Darden, "Challenged by Their Differences," *The Disciple* (August 1986): 15.

[24]Torres, *Struggle,* 83.

6

Autonomy, Equality, Relationship

Values Collide and Coalesce from 1976–Present

The last twenty-five years of the twentieth century functioned mostly as a time for the three racial-ethnic ministries to grow into the vision established in 1969, but there were no small number of growing pains.

Within the Asian American community, two major events occurred in this period. In 1976, Wilshire Korean Christian Church in southern California became the first Korean Disciples congregation, a major first for a community whose make-up is currently about 75 percent Korean.[1] In 1977, Luz Bacerra went to work for the Department of Church Women, becoming the first person of Asian ancestry to work in general offices of the church.[2]

> In 1978, out of the prophetic visions of Harold Johnson, Executive of Evangelism at Division of Homeland Ministries, the first consultation on Asian ministries was held in Indianapolis … The purpose was three-fold: to affirm the unique identity of Asian American Disciples;

to raise the consciousness among Disciples of their presence; and to help Disciples attend to the needs of the growing Asian American population.[3]

It is easy to see how this newest immigrant group within the Disciples was following in the path toward independence and equality within the denomination, just as African Americans and Latinos had before them.

Each racial-ethnic ministry remained in the mostly White church out of a commitment to unity. So it's not surprising that at some point, the groups began to seek opportunities to work together as their movements' concerns converged. By late 1978, a Committee on Black and Hispanic Concerns developed. Its initial goals were empowering an affirmative action officer for the Christian Church (Disciples of Christ) and creating more relevant church literature for Spanish-speaking congregations. According to an article at the time:

[David] Vargas [co-chair of the committee] indicated a need for blacks and Hispanics "to get to know each other better, share expertise, build positive images and develop common strategies for church growth."

Although some black and Hispanic members questioned lumping concerns together, majority opinion agreed "the committee was the only current structure for making concerns known to the church, and that it should be continued."

"The committee has viability for Hispanics until we can create our own structures," a Hispanic member stated.

"Although we share dreams, hopes and aspirations, we differ in identities, experiences and culture," said a black committee member. "Lumping us together dilutes our effectiveness."

The committee reviews church work related to blacks and Hispanics and programs of administrative units to assure minority inclusion.[4]

There would be decades of efforts to create relationships and also make clear to the general church the distinctiveness of these groups, sometimes more effectively and sometimes less. It would be a number of years before Asian American Disciples would be in a place to be a part of this conversation, with mixed results. At this point in history, however, Asian American Disciples had only just been formally acknowledged as a racial-ethnic ministry at the 1979 General Assembly.[5] While John Compton served as the first African American regional minister to the Indiana region from 1979–81,[6] American Asian Disciples held their first convocation in 1980 in Indianapolis with sixteen Asians and three General Office staff members.[7]

The intersection of cultures for Asian Americans gave birth to powerful ministries of reconciliation. The founding of American Asian Disciples is one of those stories. Soongook Choi, a Korean minister, and David Kagiwada, a Japanese-American minister, came together across all the traditional hostilities between their cultures, offering a model for reconciliation that would serve their reconciliation work with the larger church. Soongook Choi, a Korean War veteran and one of the few survivors from his platoon, brought countless Koreans into the Disciples community. He emphasized the distinctiveness of Disciples as relating to its foundation in the wholeness and healing of the body of Christ. In his own words, "To serve my neighbors and give them the impression to love, to have peace, to practice forgiveness, to produce reconciliation is my way of serving God."[8]

Speaking of his two years in a concentration camp in Poston, Arizona, Kagiwada commented: "There is a Japanese cultural quality that says 'It can't be helped.' But I'm rooted in the American tradition of the freedom of the individual, so I get irate about it and ask how it could happen."[9] Noting that German and Italian-Americans did not experience the same thing, he said, "I believe this process of misidentification is endemic to American society and continues as we compete economically with Japan. Japanese-Americans get attacked. I see it as an inability to accept nonwhite persons as fully American." But rather than using those experiences to fuel justified anger, the Rev. Kagiwada chose a path of both justice and relationship: he pastored in predominantly Anglo congregations and nurtured Anglos (particularly females) into ministry themselves; he served as first convener of Asian American Disciples (AAD) and did intentional reconciliation work between Japanese and Koreans. He also worked with Hispanic, Asian, and Black Disciples leaders to foster multiethnic Christian education in 1985. In his search and call papers in 1985, the Rev. Kagiwada acknowledged his gifts (uncharacteristically for so humble a man) in the following way:

> I believe my ministerial style to be one that enables a bridging of diversity both personality wise and theological. My strengths are in creative programming and giving persons a sense of pastoral support. I believe in a facilitating style of working with others in partnership (laity, other clergy, ecumenical). Ministry is set in a global perspective, sensitive to the diversity in the world. While I believe that the Gospel is always moving us out beyond where we are, my inclination is to be pastoral, that is, working with people where they are, supportive of their human situation.[10]

The attitudes and values of these leaders would help shape the purpose of Asian ministries for decades to come.

Not long after the first AAD convocation, the "Hispanic Encounter" found a permanent form:

> Finally, on June 24–26, 1981, the first assembly of the National Hispanic and Bilingual Fellowship took place at the Downey Avenue Christian Church in Indianapolis, Indiana. Under the theme "Somos Uno"– "Creciendo para Testimonio en Unidad y Amor" ("We Are One–Growing for Witness in Unity and Love"). More than 300 delegates representing 24 Hispanic congregations and other components of the church

came together to give formal shape to the National Hispanic and Bilingual Fellowship of the Christian Church (Disciples of Christ) in the United States and Canada.[11]

Their goals of the gathering were as follows:

To intensify the unity of the Hispanic component within the Christian Church (Disciples of Christ) in the United States and Canada and through its structure seek to bring unity to the efforts of the Hispanic and bilingual conventions, and churches and the office of Program Services to Hispanic and Bilingual Congregations of the Division of Homeland Ministries,

To intensify and provide for more effective participation and contribution by Hispanics in the activities, projects, and programs at the general level of the denomination through the development of a vehicle for communication that would serve to speak collectively, presenting the needs, problems, preoccupations, and virtues of Hispanics in general,

To intensify the communication among Hispanics and other ethnic groups within and outside the context of the Christian Church (Disciples of Christ),

To intensify the communication among Hispanic churches and the church in other parts of the world.[12]

These ministry goals represented the self-respect Latino Disciples ministers were emphasizing in their own communities. A particularly remarkable example was the ministry now known as Good Samaritans ministries, led by Feliberto Pereira and headquartered at the Christian Church in Los Fresnos, Texas. The Good Samaritans ministries started in 1971 with help from Homeland Ministries and the Southwest Region; by the early 1980s Pereira's ministry was financially poor but spiritually thriving:

Even though we live in one of the poorest economic areas of the United States, and the majority of our members receive a very low income, our church turned from being a dependent church to a self-respecting and self-supporting church. In 1981 our income was $84,000.[13]

One of the things we teach our members is to be proud of being a Christian, as well as a Hispanic member of society. We seek to help all to discover themselves as persons of value and worth in Christ and to be proud of who they are in Christ.[14]

Following his regional ministry in Indiana, John Compton became the first Black president of a general unit, heading the Division of Homeland Ministries. One of his earliest speeches in that office indicated that he did not sacrifice his core convictions in order to serve in that office. In an address to the International Christian Men's Fellowship in June 1982, he said: "Peace will not come in the world until the needs of people are addressed adequately. Peace and happiness will never be ours to claim as long as life's less fortunate discover that peace and justice pass them by. The church in the next decade will be facing a number of serious issues which have brought the world to the 'razor's' edge of disaster—hunger, displaced persons, children, the poor, racism and sexism."[15] Compton, who had engaged in radical civil rights work in the 1960s and continued his commitment to justice throughout his life, served as a leader and model for the next generation of justice advocates within the Disciples.

In seemingly unrelated events, Haitians fleeing the oppression of the Duvalier regime flooded into New York; and thousands were helped by the Evangelical Crusade Christian Church, founded in 1973. "We had over 1,000 beds in the church hallways," said the pastor. "We dedicate ourselves to service. Not just the spiritual, but social service as well. We treat the whole person. The Haitian population is growing in New York. Some come here to worship, some come here to have their needs met. They know that we are here for them twenty-four hours a day, every day."[16] This racial-ethnic ministry would begin to grow rapidly, but at this point was still very much under the radar of most Disciples.

The committee on Black and Hispanic Concerns continued to meet. Under its new name, the Committee for Racial-Ethnic Inclusiveness and Empowerment, it brought a resolution to the 1987 General Assembly. At this point, they also invited representatives from the Asian American community to participate.

The distinctive gatherings of Latino, African American and Asian American racial-ethnic ministries frustrated some Anglo Americans within the Disciples. Those frustrated felt that the purpose of the church was unity, and that these ethnic groups divided the church. Maureen Osuga, a leader in the Asian American community, explained the need for these types of gatherings in the following way:

> My feelings of being a Japanese person—feelings that lie at the core of my sense of myself, my view of reality, and my values—lay outside my experience of and participation in the church. None of the churches in my life included me in any overt, positive way. Hence I was included on their terms, and my "Japaneseness" was nonessential and invisible. I was not invited to share that part of myself, nor did it occur to me to offer. As I think back, to have pushed myself into those churches would have violated that inner sense of needing to be invited in as an outsider.
>
> Until David Kagiwada and Grace Kim recruited me into the American Asian Disciples group around 1977, some of the richest, most important parts of my sense of self lay outside my experience of church. Every time I am with AAD again, when the milieu of worship and interaction have a distinctively Asian flavor, I experience a deep sense of connection and presence

to myself and others that has become increasingly important to me as a Disciple. I do not believe my experience is unusual. Most AAD members are in white churches. We all struggle daily to hold onto important parts of ourselves, and we breathe a sigh of relief and joy when we have a chance to be together, even if for two short days.[17]

In some ways, these gatherings gave strength and assurance to people of color who functioned for much of their Christian lives in an Anglo church with an Anglo ethos. It refueled them so that they would have the energy to do the work of Christian unity that kept them in the church in the first place.

As with African Americans (1960) and Latinos (1970), the General Assembly created a position within the Division of Homeland Ministries to focus exclusively on American Asian ministries in 1991. This generated some conflict, with many of the same concerns raised as had been raised when Homeland Ministries began to move toward self-appointed leadership for the Latino community. Soongook Choi described an initial meeting in 1989:

I recall to my chagrin the general atmosphere with regard to Asian ministries was at best lukewarm with many hesitations and reluctances, although there were a few positive signs. There were hesitations understandably about investing mission energy into an 'ethnic' or 'language-specific' ministry because it might develop into a divisive element within the church. There were reluctances because it could arouse jealousy among 'other Asian-language peoples.'[18]

Finally, Homeland Ministries hired Geunhee Yu in 1992, who continues to serve as Executive Pastor for North American Pacific and Asian Disciples (NAPAD). At the time of his arrival, there were eight Asian American Disciples churches.[19] By 2000, that number had grown to seventy.[20]

While Asian Disciples had reached a milestone in their journey toward inclusion and equal standing within the Christian Church (Disciples of Christ), some African American leaders raised questions and concerns about how far the White church was really willing to go on that journey. When Black Disciples formally merged with White Disciples in 1969, they did so with clear goals for the achievement of equality and a fundamental commitment to racial justice. In 1991, Samuel Hylton, one of the most prominent Black Disciples leaders, shared the following theological concerns about how White Disciples were approaching their commitments to both justice and covenant:

> The fundamental principle which holds the Christian Church (Disciples of Christ) together is the concept of covenant. The covenantal relationship binds us as a people to God and to each other. I personally believe that the refusal of Texas Christian University to divest its funds from South Africa when the General Assembly asked church organizations to do so was a violation of covenant.
>
> The question is: Are autonomy and covenant compatible principles? How do we as a church live out mission, witness and service in wholeness as long as a manifestation of the church chooses to ignore a principle, program, priority on a goal just because it has a right to do so under our polity?
>
> Frankly as I read the Bible and reflect on the life and teaching of Jesus, I find more support for the principle of covenant than I do for the principle of autonomy. As we look forward to the 21st century, our challenge as a church, is in creating a sense of unity and common purpose.
>
> What is needed in the church not only in racial matters, but in all programmatic areas, is the capacity to think not in terms of what is good for any

given manifestation, but what is good for the whole church.[21]

Black Disciples leaders continued to raise similar questions as they wrestled with what they had gained and what they had lost in the merger. In a 2005 interview, Raymond Brown stated that he had absolutely no regrets about his role in merging the National Convention into the International Convention because of the biblical goal of unity in the body of Christ. His only regret was how little Black Disciples had gained in that merger because of the continuing racism within the church.[22]

The Disciples' General Assembly in Charlotte, North Carolina, in 2003 served a historic function: it offered an opportunity for reconciliation between the historic Black churches of the District Assemblies in North Carolina and along the eastern seaboard and the General Assembly of the Christian Church (Disciples of Christ). After conversations had broken down in the 1950s and 1960s (with accusations of strong-arm tactics), countless Disciples leaders (including Emmett Dickson, J.O. Williams, Alvin Jackson, Valerie Melvin and Sotello Long) engaged in the hard work of healing and reconciliation. The story of the Assembly churches' rich blessings for the rest of the Christian Church (Disciples of Christ) is yet to be completed.

Beyond the challenges of functioning in a predominantly-Anglo communion, racial-ethnic ministries faced very real challenges around identity issues within their own ministries. Flagship La Hermosa Christian Church reflected the struggles of many Latino Disciples churches in this period, a struggle that many Asian Disciples churches would grow into as their immigrant populations stabilized as well:

> Mr. Sanchez [pastor of La Hermosa CC for seven years] has seen his church's membership fluctuate as people relocate back and forth to Puerto Rico. The membership presently [in 1986] stands at 150.
>
> "Pretty soon we are going to have to make some decisions about whether to continue conducting the

services in Spanish," says Mr. Sanchez. "We have new
members coming in from Central America who don't
understand English. But our children are growing up
and they are going to schools that stress English. So
now we have children who don't speak Spanish. Right
now we teach the children's church school in English
and worship in Spanish, but we won't be able to do it
forever," he says.

"Our church is in a neighborhood where real estate
is getting extremely expensive. Then the poor move
out, the buildings are upgraded and, of course, so are
the rents. It is impossible to find an apartment that rents
for less than $500 a month. We are supposed to have
rent control here but the only control I see is control
over the poor," he says.[23]

As Hispanic Disciples struggled with the challenges within
their own communities, they began to wrestle with their needs
and their place within the larger Disciples body. As the General
Assembly created an Asian American ministries position in
1991, Latino Disciples decided they needed a level of autonomy
that the existing church structures could not afford them. They
also removed themselves from the Committee for Racial-Ethnic
Inclusiveness and Empowerment, citing a need to focus on
internal issues for the immediate future. As they moved in this
direction, they talked about their history of communication
struggles with the White church through different venues. In
one article in *The Disciple,* a Latino leader wrote:

In North American institutions, bureaucracy and for-
mality are important factors for communication. That
understanding of life fails to meet the expectation
of Hispanics. From the Hispanic perspective these
institutions and understandings of reality give the
impression of a cold, impersonal people. Latin American society is a face-to-face-oriented community. If the
church wants to serve the Hispanic population in the

United States, that must be understood. Hispanics will not respond to a "business-like" understanding of faith with its bureaucratic and often impersonal attitude.[24]

In their proposal to move from Homeland Ministries into their own office, they offered the following reflection:

> Embracing the slogan, "Somos Uno," (We are One), the Hispanic and Bilingual Fellowship of the Christian Church wrote the following in their 1991 Project for the Creation of a Central Pastoral Office for Hispanic Ministries (approved by the General Board and then given almost no funding the following year by the Finance Commission):
>
> As an offering of integrity, we share the testimony of a people who are sure that in order to serve God and to spread the Good News of Salvation of our Lord Jesus Christ, it is possible to do it from a Hispanic idiosyncrasy, without having to separate or dislodge oneself from the ecclesiastical principles and politics of the Disciples of Christ. In other words, we reaffirm on these pages, not only our conviction that we are ONE as a Hispanic family, but our sincere desire and goal to be truly ONE with the whole Disciples Church and the Church of Christ universally.[25]

The move was financially challenging, and the financial support from the general church was found by the Pastoral Commission to be an "offense to the dignity of Hispanic Disciples."[26]

As they reflected on the process that had brought them to this point, the Hispanic Caucus wrote:

> For Hispanic Disciples, the past four years of pilgrimage have been exciting, but also painful. During that pilgrimage, we have frequently encountered either the indifference or clear opposition of some key persons in general units, regions, and other organizations of the church; and we cannot deny their right to

do so. Since our project has clearly established that regions and general units have failed to address our needs and have been unable to serve effectively our constituency for almost 100 years, there are, of course, obvious reasons for some of them to react negatively to our proposal. However, what we do perceive as a clear injustice is the attempt of some of them to use their power, influence and access to decision-making levels in order to systematically discredit and block our journey. In some instances, such maneuvers have occurred "confidentially" behind our backs, while at the same time those offices and individuals have shown our constituency a "supportive" façade. For us, such behavior has been very difficult to face, to decipher, and especially to accept, but we were always sustained by the hope that justice would prevail. However, it did not.[27]

David Vargas, current president of the Division of Overseas Ministries, wrote during this time about Hispanic Disciples' sense of serving as tokens but not as partners–with the dominant community valuing them only for their existing numbers and not their potential:

We feel that the cry of our Hispanic people in the United States (inside as well as outside the church) is not a serious priority for the Disciples. The church responds to our need based on the proportion we represent within the total Disciples membership, rather than based on what we, with the support of all of the church, are called to be and do in response to the challenge that our Hispanic nation presents for this country. Considering this challenge, we are no longer talking about 65 churches/missions and close to 6,000 members, but rather about 20 million persons who, in the richest country of the world, suffer the consequences of racism, exploitation, hunger and many other social evils.[28]

For more than 90 years, Hispanic Disciples have been recipients of programs and projects that are designed by non-Hispanics or persons who are foreign to our pilgrimage, and based on priorities and projections that are not ours. Now that we have come to a place of being able to design, implement, and be the main actors in our destiny, we hoped to be able to count on the support and accompaniment of those who used to do the programming for us. But the reality is another: not only are we missing that support, but we feel that due to the budgetary deficit that we confront, we are now pressured to spend our time and energy begging for resources from various units and other offices of the church.[29]

We feel that although we are constantly used for purposes of promotion and public relations, when it comes to distributing the resources of our church, it does not respond with the same intensity. Inclusivity in our church is basically a public relations exercise. Church reports, special offering promotions and other materials that are often published with the objective of demonstrating our church's commitment to justice, equality, compassion, etc., frequently contain photographs and descriptions that give the impression that Hispanics are an integral part of the dynamic of our denomination. However, this is only in terms of public relations. In those photographs, for instance, we frequently appear as one among five or six people or images. Nevertheless, in terms of programmatic and budgetary support the percentage is much less. In the Bethany decision, for example, the percentage was less than one in one hundred.[30]

Disciples historian Daisy Machado also shared in 1997 firsthand experiences of this ministry on the margins within the Disciples church:

> In our eleven-year ministry we were evicted from one Disciples church facility because the congregation decided they didn't want any more "Mexicans" in their building. Another Disciples congregation agreed to let us use their facility but we were forbidden from bringing our children into the nursery because 'the mothers were concerned that Hispanic children carried lice.' In our most recent new church start, which is three years old, we were advised by regional staff to work with 'educated assimilated Hispanics' because poor Hispanics 'can't give the money that is needed to get a new church going.'[31]

After mentioning that she had spoken at General Assembly, many regional and Disciples' women and youth events, and has served on General Board and Board for Disciples Historical Society, Machado continued:

> Yet my pastoral ministry, which began in 1978, has always taken place on the fringes of both this denomination and this society. Perhaps this surprises you. How can an individual be so close yet so far? And this very paradox of belonging yet not really belonging where the history of Latinos within the Disciples begins to be understood. It is also where we need to begin our analysis of what this paradox implies for the Disciples in the twenty-first century.[32]

While there is much hope for Asian Americans in the Christian Church's future, Dr. Yu (along with many Asian American Disciples) finds it disheartening that in the context of this history, many Asian Disciples experience a mixed message regarding welcome at the Table. He writes:

Most of the Asian Disciples congregations are in a 'nesting' relationship, sharing a facility with the European American churches for their ministry. Many of the Asian churches have to suffer unnecessary hardships due to the mixed message of the church. Many other Disciples churches, for the worse, do not even open their doors to the latecomers like Asian Americans. It means a welcome table in a closed church. Isn't this an oxymoron for our church?[33]

Chapters continue to be written about the journey of people of color in the Christian Church (Disciples of Christ). As part of the new church movement, churches of color make up almost two-thirds of new churches. Newer immigrant communities like Mongolians and Haitians are finding their way into a denomination that is increasingly equipped to embrace them for who they are, not simply welcoming them to try to become part of a dominant culture. The denomination's commitment to anti-racism bubbles up from local congregations and also infuses the way general units approach ministry. It offers possibilities for meeting communities of color on their own terms and moving from the need for autonomy toward covenant and greater cooperation, rather than suppression within the dominant body.

Other chapters are still unwritten, but space will open up at the Table for all, with equal access to all of its riches, if we choose to know and acknowledge our history and intentionally work toward the biblical mandate of honoring one another in our diversity. May we all someday be able not just to eat at the Welcome Table with elbow room for all; but may we also be able to share our dishes with one another and have that banquet of diversity be greatly received by all.

Notes

[1]Geunhee Yu, "Asian American Disciples," in *The Encyclopedia of the Stone-Campbell Movement,* ed. Douglas A. Foster, Paul M. Blowers, Anthony

L Dunnavant, and D. Newell Williams (Grand Rapids, Mich.: William B. Eerdmans, 2004), 40.

[2]Janet Casey-Allen, "Disciples of Asian origin vie for their place," *The Disciple* (May 1994): 9.

[3]Yu, "Asian American Disciples," 39.

[4]"Committee on Black and Hispanic Concerns Sets Goals," *The Disciple* (March 4, 1979): 20.

[5]Yu, "Asian American Disciples," 39.

[6]Robert L. Friedly, "The way paver," *The Disciple* (June 1991): 4.

[7]Yu, "Asian American Disciples," 2.

[8]Undated Soongook Choi scholarship brochure from Disciples Home Missions.

[9]Sally Wright, "David Kagiwada: Japanese and American heritages shape ministry," *The Disciple* (August 1984): 7.

[10]David Kagiwada, Relocation Assistance Form [search and call], March 28, 1985.

[11]David Vargas, "A Historical Background of the National Hispanic and Bilingual Fellowship," *Discipliana* 46 (Fall 1986): 42.

[12]Ibid.

[13]F. Feliberto Pereira, "Church Expanding," *The Disciple* (April 17, 1983): 10.

[14]Ibid., 11.

[15]"The Legacy of God's Four Horsemen," *The Oldtimers' Grapevine* (October-December 2005): 2.

[16]Londia R. Darden, "Challenged by Their Differences," *The Disciple* (August 1986): 15.

[17]Rita Nakashima Brock, "Asian Americans need second invitation," *The Disciple* (July 1987): 60.

[18]Soongook Choi, "Korean Disciples: Embodying Pentecost," *The Disciple* (May 1994): 4–5.

[19]Yu, "Asian American Disciples," 3.

[20]Ibid., 40.

[21]Samuel W. Hylton, Jr, "Accountability to covenant: A black pastor calls Disciples beyond autonomy to responsibility," *The Disciple* (June 1991): 19.

[22]That interview has since been lost due to recording device failure. This is based on the interviewer's memory of the conversation.

[23]Londia R. Darden, "Challenged by Their Differences," *The Disciple* (August 1986): 16.

[24]Samuel Pagán, "Hispanics and the Church," *The Disciple* (September 1990): 29.

[25]"Project for the Creation of a Central Pastoral Office for Hispanic Ministries, Christian Church (Disciples of Christ) in the United States and Canada, revised according to what was approved by the General Board in Chicago, Illinois, on July 29, 1991."

[26]Hispanic Caucus, National Hispanic and Bilingual Fellowship, "Wanting Disciples to celebrate their growth: Hispanic Disciples feel betrayed," *The Disciple* (August 1992): 24.

[27]Ibid.

[28]David Vargas, "Hispanic effort is on behalf of whole church," *The Disciple* (August 1992): 25.

[29]Ibid.

[30]Ibid.

[31]Daisy Machado, "From Ango-American [sic] Traditions to a Multicultural World," *Discipliana* 57 (Summer 1997), 48.

[32]Ibid., 47.

[33]Yu, "Asian American Disciples," 3.

Conclusion

The Christian Church (Disciples of Christ) began as a primitivist movement or a restorationist movement, striving to reestablish a mythic New Testament Church. In the process, the founders denied the social context into which the Disciples Movement was birthed.

Today, the church is expanding and diversifying rapidly. The early church reminds us of the tensions and conflicts we will face. Most of Paul's letters were written in response to cultural as well as theological differences between different groups trying to unite despite a not-always-unified understanding of God in Christ.

Today we face similar challenges: as new church ministry explodes among people of color, the face of the church is changing. As churches in transformation reconnect with their communities, they are realizing that their potential members (those living in the neighborhood) are considerably more diverse than their existing membership.

The church has to decide what is essential and what is nonessential as it tries to live out its claim that the Table belongs to Christ and not to us. In the past, many people of color who were drawn to this tradition were drawn with a commitment to Christian unity and to a faith that allowed for differences in belief. The tragedy of our history is that we do not tend to dwell on the differences between our groups because we consciously or unconsciously categorize them as nonessentials, thereby treating them as if they should not be discussed—we agree to disagree and avoid the conversation.

But the stories of people of color in the Disciples are not simply stories. They are indicators of our theology and our Christian ethics—what we understand about God and relating to one another in light of our relationship with God. The essential in this history is that God demands that all people receive equal dignity. The essential is that if we have a Welcome Table, there should be no privileged places. Everyone should have the chance to eat and talk.

Throughout our history we have pretended to confuse the essential of equal dignity in Christ with the nonessential of worship style(or whatever else we think makes our groups different). Our history books point out almost with pride that our church did not divide over the issue of slavery as others did, thinking that this "political" issue was a nonessential rather than an essential. During World War II, our publications noted that we got the essential right–offering kindness to Japanese Americans being sent to internment camps–instead of thinking that the essential was defending the basic human dignity that all people deserved. We could remain united during that time because we did not allow the nonessential–our understandings of how the U.S. government should treat Japanese Americans–get in the way of the essential issue, sharing God's mercy. The mercy we shared, though, was a mercy without justice. And mercy without justice is not essential in God's mind (see Micah 6:8).

Another error that the church makes repeatedly is the distinction between private and public, as if such a distinction can be made. Thomas Campbell never argued it was wrong for slaves to be slaves; but he did recognize it was wrong for them to be deprived of the spiritual sustenance of reading the Bible and hearing the Word of God. Campbell demanded that slaves be given the opportunities to study the gospel and to preach it, thus violating state laws in some instances, but he did not demand that they be freed. Disciples were determined to share God's love with Japanese interned during World War II, but were not determined to speak out against the mistreatment. They established a Chinese mission; but as its numbers dwindled, they never questioned the validity of the Chinese Exclusion Act. Making religion private has hurt the people God called us to advocate for, and it has hurt us as a denomination.

Disciples at our best have embraced dialogue across vast divides, allowing people of diverse beliefs around the Table (starting with Stone the Unitarian and Campbell the Trinitarian). Too often, however, people of good will have been lulled into thinking that tolerance and justice are identical. As our denomination claims a different sort of pioneering spirit in the twenty-first century, let us recognize the communitarian values of our immigrant histories. With these values we can equip ourselves better to resist the oppression of the people at the Table, empowering one another as parts of the whole body of Christ.

Personal Copy
Jerry McAllister

Time Line of Disciples History

1801   The Cane Ridge Camp Meeting brings together Christians from different sects in an enthusiastic expression of ecumenical worship.

1804   Barton Stone, inspired by the ecumenism and spirit of the Cane Ridge Revival, gathers with several other Presbyterian ministers to write "The Last Will and Testament of the Springfield Presbytery," with the goal of forming a "primitive" church unified as one body.

1809   Thomas Campbell (father of Alexander Campbell) gathers Christians from several denominations for Christian worship. They form the Christian Association of Washington in Washington County, Pennsylvania.

1820   African American members are listed in records of churches in Cane Ridge, Kentucky and Brush Run, Pennsylvania.

1832   Barton Stone's "Christian Movement" and Alexander Campbell's "Disciples Movement" join together in Lexington, Kentucky.

1834   Colored Christian Church is instituted. African Americans in mixed congregations are welcome to serve as "exhorters"–preachers to other African Americans, deacons who serve other African Americans, and custodians. In Black churches they can serve in all roles. Congregations are generally autonomous in free states; in slave states, they and their officers are supervised by a White "mother church."

1849   The American Christian Missionary Society (ACMS) is constituted to "promote the gospel in destitute places of our own and foreign lands."

1851   James Barkley is sent to Jerusalem as first Disciples missionary.

1853   Alexander Cross, recognized for his great preaching, is bought out of slavery to become first Disciples missionary to Liberia. (Cross dies soon after his arrival, probably of malaria.)

1874   The Christian Woman's Board of Mission (CWBM) is established.

1875   The Foreign Christian Missionary Society (FCMS) is established.

1875   Southern Christian Institute (SCI) is chartered by the state of Mississippi to offer education and trade skills to free Blacks.

1882   The CWBM and the FCMS establishes a mission in India.

1882   Southern Christian Institute (SCI) opens its doors. It merges into Tougaloo College in 1954. (SCI is one of only three Disciples-established Black higher education institutions at the end of the nineteenth century.)

1883   The CWBM and FCMS establish a mission in Japan.

1886   The CWBM and FCMS establish a mission in China.

1887   The Christian Church (Disciples of Christ) establishes the National Benevolent Association (NBA)to help consolidate its charitable efforts within the United States.

1891   The CWBM opens a Chinese mission in Portland, Oregon.

1893   Disciples participate in a land grab in Oklahoma to establish churches for pioneers. The land grab displaces thousands of Native Americans.

1897   The CWBM and the FCMS establish a mission in what is now the Congo.

1899   The ACMS approves first Spanish-language Christian Church in San Antonio. The church disbanded in 1905, and Guy Inman and Felipe Jiménez reorganized it in 1908. [Note: 1904-1927 sees the start of eleven new Latino churches, four started by Latinos themselves]

1899 The CWBM and the FCMS establish a mission in Cuba.

1900 The CWBM and the FCMS establish a mission in Hawaii.

1906 Churches of Christ break from the Disciples around issues including scriptural authority and instrumental music.

1907 The Christian Churches approved membership in Federal Council of Churches (eventually known as the National Council of Churches.

1907 CWBM starts the Chinese Christian Institute in San Francisco.

1908 Japanese Christian Church is established in Los Angeles.

1910 The Disciples ecumenical ministry, Council on Christian Unity, is established.

1913 The Inman Center is established to house Mexican Americans in San Antonio.

1914 A Japanese students' Bible group in Berkeley, California that started in 1904 formalizes itself as Berkeley Japanese Christian Church.

1916 First records of State Mexican Convention. They continued until 1922, and resumed again in 1944 with seven churches in Texas participating.

1917 International Convention of Disciples is established

1917 National Christian Missionary Convention (NCMC) establishes African American Disciples with Preston Taylor as its leader "to create a medium of self-expression and cooperative endeavor for development of our churches that our best contribution may be made to our posterity and to the world." It is established largely to give autonomy to Black Disciples churches, who had been placed into a "parent-child" relationship with White churches.

1919 United Christian Missionary Society is created to consolidate mission work among Disciples

1921 Yakima (now Yakama) Mission for Native Americans is opened after a year of building by the ACMS.

1923   Chinese missions close as Chinese populations dwindle as a result of the Chinese Exclusion Acts and anti-Asian hostility.

1933   Filipino Christian Church is founded in Los Angeles (still in existence).

1935   Disciples Peace Fellowship is established.

1939   La Hermosa Christian Church is established. It becomes the first Hispanic Disciples church in New York in 1943 when it affiliates.

1942   With the internment of Japanese people, Japanese Christian Church in Los Angeles is taken under care by denomination—All Peoples Christian Center is born. At the end of the war, some Japanese Americans return to the building and what is now All Peoples. Others desire their own church back.1944—The NCMC votes to expand its partnership with the United Christian Missionary Society. Arguably beginning the process that leads to the merger in 1969, the merger is completed in 1960.

1948   Although there were four Japanese Disciples churches before World War II, the denomination finally agrees to help build another one, West Adams Christian Church in Los Angeles after the war (after efforts to assimilate all Japanese Disciples into existing congregations), giving birth to West Adams Christian Church (still in existence) in Los Angeles.

1958   Second Christian Church in the Bronx hosts the first Northwest Convention of Hispanic Christian Churches (Disciples of Christ) involving six congregations.

1960   Commission on Brotherhood Restructure is authorized, beginning the movement toward the Disciples' official establishment as a denomination.

1965   The Immigration Act opens the United States' borders to Asian immigrants, creating opportunities for ministry in Asian American community.

1966   Division of Homeland Ministries (DHM) organizes Consultation on Hispanic Ministry, including Hispanic

American leaders and leaders from Mexico and Puerto Rico.

1968 Christian Church (Disciples of Christ) officially becomes a denomination, and many Independent Christian Churches/Churches of Christ choose not to affiliate with it. "Provisional Design of the Christian Church" is adopted at this time.

1969 The International Convention of Christian Churches adopts "Principles for Merger of the National Christian Missionary Convention and the International Convention of Christian Churches (Disciples of Christ)," completing twenty-six years of movement toward unity between African American and White Disciples.

1969 DHM calls Domingo Rodríguez as first Hispanic to serve as Director of the Office of Programs and Services for Hispanic and Bilingual Congregations, replacing Byron Spice.

1970 Domingo Rodriguez, Director of Program Services to Hispanic Congregations at DHM leads the first conference of Hispanic American Ministers in Indianapolis, including thirty-eight ministers from eleven states, Mexico, and Puerto Rico.

1972 Harold Johnson of DHM visits Thailand and begins to realize the need to foster conversation among Asian Disciples in the United States.

1976 Wilshire Korean Christian Church becomes first Korean Disciples congregation (Korean Disciples represent 75% of NAPAD congregations).

1977 Luz Bacerra is hired by Department of Church Women, becoming the first person of Asian ancestry to work in the general church.

1978 Midwest Hispanic and Bilingual Convention of Christian Churches meets for the first time.

1978 Harold Johnson calls the first consultation of Asian Disciples (including sixteen Asians and three general church staff members).

1979   John Compton becomes the first African American to serve as Regional Minister (Indiana, 1979-81)

1979   "The Hispanic Encounter" is established to welcome laypeople into what had previously been a Hispanic ministers group.

1979   AAD (American Asian Disciples) formally acknowledged as a racial-ethnic ministry (with formal recognition by General Board in 1984).

1982   John Compton becomes first African American to serve as president of a General Unit (DHM, 1982-1989).

1990   After sixty-seven years, Chinese Disciples ministries begin again with First Christian Church in Alhambra, California.

1991   General Assembly directs DHM to create a position to focus exclusively on Asian American Ministries. Dr. Geunhee Yu is called to the position in 1992, when there are eight American Asian Disciples congregations.

1992   Central Pastoral Office on Hispanic Ministries is established as an independent organization within the general church.

2005   Sharon Watkins named first female head of a mainline denomination.

Personal Copy
Jerry McAllister